Women Explorers

Alexandra David-Néel
Explorer at the Roof of the World

Women Explorers

Women Explorers

Alexandra David-Néel
Explorer at the Roof of the World

Earle Rice Jr.

Introduction: Milbry Polk,
author of *Women of Discovery*

CHELSEA HOUSE
PUBLISHERS
A Haights Cross Communications Company
Philadelphia

CHELSEA HOUSE PUBLISHERS
VP, NEW PRODUCT DEVELOPMENT Sally Cheney
DIRECTOR OF PRODUCTION Kim Shinners
CREATIVE MANAGER Takeshi Takahashi
MANUFACTURING MANAGER Diann Grasse

Staff for ALEXANDRA DAVID-NÉEL
ASSOCIATE EDITOR Kate Sullivan
PHOTO EDITOR Sarah Bloom
PRODUCTION EDITOR Megan Emery
SERIES & COVER DESIGNER Terry Mallon
LAYOUT 21st Century Publishing and Communications, Inc.

A Haights Cross Communications Company

http://www.chelseahouse.com

First Printing

9 8 7 6 5 4 3 2 1

Library of Congress Cataloging-in-Publication Data

Rice, Earle.
   Alexandra David-Neel: explorer at the roof of the world/by Earle Rice, Jr.
     p. cm.
Includes index.
   ISBN 0-7910-7715-2
   1. Tibet (China)—Description and travel—Juvenile literature. 2. David-Neel,
Alexandra, 1868-1969—Travel—China—Tibet—Juvenile literature. I. Title:
Explorer at the roof of the world. II. Title.
DS785.R52 2004
915.1'50441—dc22

                                                          2003026135

Table of Contents

Introduction

By Milbry Polk

Curiosity is one of the most compelling forces of human life. Our desire to understand who and what and where we are drives us restlessly to explore and to comprehend what we see. Every historical era is known by the individuals who sought to expand our boundaries of time and space and knowledge. People such as Alexander the Great, Ibn Battuta, Marco Polo, Ferdinand Magellan, Hernando de Soto, Meriwether Lewis, William Clark, Charles Darwin, Sir Richard Burton, Roald Amundsen, Jacques Cousteau, Edmund Hillary, Tenzing Norgay, Thor Hyerdahl, and Neil Armstrong are men whose discoveries changed our worldview. They were explorers, leaders into the unknown. This series is about a handful of individuals who have been left out of the history books but whose feats loom large, whose discoveries changed the way we look at the world. They are women explorers.

WHAT MAKES SOMEONE AN EXPLORER?

The desire to know what lies beyond the next hill—the desire to explore—is one of the most powerful of human impulses. This drive makes us unique among the species with which we share our earth. Curiosity helped to impel our remote ancestors out of Africa. It is what spread them in waves throughout the world where they settled; curiosity helped them adapt to the many environments they encountered.

Myths of all cultures include the memories of early explorations. These myths were the means by which people explained to themselves and taught their children about life, about the world around them, and about death. Myths helped people make sense of the inexplicable forces of nature and the strangeness of new lands and peoples. The few myths and legends that have come down to us are the stories of early exploration.

What makes someone an explorer? The qualities required are not unique. We are born explorers. Every child, even in the crib, is reaching out, trying to understand, to take the measure of its own body, then its immediate surroundings, and we continue as we go through life to grasp ever-widening circles of experience and reality. As we grow up, we often lose the excitement of the child, the characteristic that supposedly gave Albert Einstein his ability to see the universe in a new way. What typifies the explorer is not losing this wonderful childlike curiosity. He or she still reaches out. Explorers are open minded—able to look at and accept what they see, rather than to fall back upon pre-conceived notions. Explorers are courageous, not just in facing physical danger, but also in having the courage to confront failure, ridicule, and laughter, and yet to keep on going. Above all, explorers have the ability to communicate. All insights, observations, and discoveries mean nothing to the wider community if they are not documented and shared. An explorer goes out into the world at some personal risk and discovers something of value and then shares that knowledge with his or her community. Explorers are leaders who look at the world in new ways and in doing so make breakthroughs that enrich all of our lives.

WOMEN EXPLORERS

Women, like men, have always been explorers. Typically in a "hunter-gatherer" society the men hunted animals while the women ventured far from the camps in search of other foods. Though their tasks were different, both were explorers. And, since such societies were almost constantly on the move, women were there for each voyage of discovery. But over time, as cultural groups became more settled, ideas began to change about the role of women in society. Women came to be restricted to the house, the shared courtyard, or the village and began to wear clothing that set them apart. By the time of the Middle Ages often the only way women in the Western world could travel was by going on pilgrimage. The trek to visit holy sites offered women one of the few opportunities to see new places, hear new languages, and meet different people. In fact, the first autobiography in the English language was written by a pilgrim, Margery Kempe (1373–1440), about her journeys throughout Europe and to the Holy Land.

Over time, women became formally excluded from exploration. Of course, some women did manage to find a way around the obstacles. Those who did venture forth went alone or in disguise and often needed men to help them. But their stories were not recorded in official histories; to find their stories one has to dig deep.

About three hundred years ago, the western worldview changed. Beginning in the 1700s, the scientific revolution began to change life for everyone in Europe. Men as well as women were swept up in the excitement to classify and understand every aspect of life on earth. Legions of people went to every corner of the world to see and record what was there. The spirit of adventure began to find new means of expression. New modes of transportation made movement around the world easier and new technologies made recording events and communication less expensive and more vivid.

The findings of these explorers were fascinating to the people back home. Wealthy individuals collected many of the strange insects, botanical specimens, native art, rocks, and other findings, brought back by the explorers into personal collections called Cabinets of Curiosities. These Cabinets of

Curiosities are the forerunners of our modern museums. The desire to collect the unusual financed expeditions, which in turn fostered public interest in exploration. The creation and spread of scientific and popular magazines with stories about expeditions and discoveries enabled the public to learn about the world. By the 1800s, explorers had the status of popular heroes in the public eye. The lure of the unknown gripped society.

Unlike men, women did not have support of institutions such as universities, museums, scientific societies, governments, and the military that sponsored and financed exploration. Until well into the twentieth century, many of these institutions barred women from participation, membership, and especially leadership. Women were thought capable of gathering things such as flowers or rocks for subjects to paint and draw, but men were the ones who studied them, named them, and published books about them. Most women, if they had any specialized education at all, gained it through private tutors. Men went to the university. Men formed and joined scientific societies and the exploring clubs. Men ran the governments, the military, and the press, and archived the collections. Universities and other cultural institutions were open only to the membership of men. Women were generally excluded from them. When these institutions sponsored exploration, they sponsored men. Women not only had to overcome mountains in the wild but also institutions at home.

In the 1800s women were not usually trained or taught academics. Instead, they learned sewing, music, and how to behave as a lady. A woman who managed to learn to write overcame great obstacles. Few managed to do it, but the same spirit that made women into explorers animated their minds in other ways. A few women learned to record what they were doing sufficiently well that at least some of their works have become classics of description and adventure.

Because of them, we know the little we do know about their lives and actions. As the nineteenth century progressed, more and more women were going out collecting, recording, and writing about faraway places. By the late 1800s more women were educated and those who traveled often wrote accounts of their journeys. So, now, in the twenty-first century, we are just beginning to learn about the unknown side of exploration—the women's story—from the accounts that lay buried in our archives.

And what a story it is. For example, one of the first modern women explorers was Maria Sybila Merian, who sailed to Surinam in 1699 at the age of 52. Not content to view the strange flora and fauna that were arriving back in Europe to fill the Cabinets of Curiosity, she wanted to collect and paint insects and animals in their native habitat.

Western women also faced societal obstacles; they generally could not go anywhere without a chaperon. So for a would-be woman explorer, a night in the wild spent in the company of a man who was not a close relative or her husband was unthinkable. And then there were the unsuitable clothes. In many parts of the early modern world it was punishable by death (as it was in Spain in the 1600s) or imprisonment (as it was in America well into the late 1800s) for women to appear in public wearing pants.

The heavy, layered dresses and tight corsets thought necessary for women made traveling very cumbersome. For example, when the Alps began to be climbed by explorers in the 1800s, a few women were caught up in the mania. The first two women to summit the Matterhorn climbed in skirts and corsets. The third woman, an American professor of Latin, Annie Smith Peck (1850–1935), realized the absurdity of leaping crevasses, climbing ice walls, and enduring the winds in a skirt. So, she wore pants. This created such a sensation in 1895 that the Singer Sewing

Machine Company photographed her and included a card with her in climbing gear with every machine it sold.

THE WOMEN EXPLORERS SERIES

When asked why he wanted to climb Mount Everest, George Mallory famously replied, "Because it's there." Perhaps another explorer would answer the same question, "Because I don't know what is there and I want to find out."

Although we all have curiosity, what separates explorers is their willingness to take their curiosity further. Despite the odds, a lack of money, and every imaginable difficulty, they still find a way to go. They do so because they are passionate about life and their passion carries them over the barriers. As you will discover, the women profiled in this series shared that passion. Their passion gave them the strength to face what would seem to be insurmountable odds to most of us. To read their stories is more than learning about the adventure, it is a guide to discovering our own passions. The women in this series, Mary Kingsley, Gertrude Bell, Alexandra David-Néel, Annie Montague Alexander, Sue Hendrickson, and Sylvia Earle, all join the pantheon of explorers, the heroes of our age.

These six women have been chosen because their interests range from geographical to cultural exploration; from traversing the highest mountains to diving to the depths of the oceans; from learning about life far back in time to looking forward into the future. These women are extraordinary leaders and thinkers. They are all individuals who have braved the unknown and challenged the traditional women's roles. Their discoveries have had remarkable and profound effects on what we know about the world. To be an explorer one does not have to be wealthy or have multiple degrees. To be an explorer one must have the desire from within and focus on the destination: the unknown.

Mary Kingsley (1862–1900) was the daughter of an English Victorian gentleman-explorer who believed women did not need to be educated. Mary was kept at home and only tutored in German to translate articles her father wanted to read. But while he was away, she went into his library and educated herself by reading his books. She never married and followed the custom of her day for unmarried women by staying home with her parents. When her parents died she found herself alone—and suddenly free. She purchased a ticket to the Canary Islands with her inheritance. Once there, she learned about the Congo, then considered by the Europeans to be a terrifying place. When Kingsley decided to go to the Congo, she was warned that all she would find would be festering swamplands laced with deadly diseases and cannibals. Kingsley viewed that warning as a challenge. Having used up all her money on the ticket, she outfitted herself as a trader. She returned to the Congo, and in a wooden canoe she plied the tributaries of the Congo River, trading goods with the natives and collecting fish for the British Museum. She learned the languages of the interior and befriended the local tribes. She became an expert on their rich belief systems, which were completely unknown in Europe. Like many explorers, Mary Kingsley's knowledge bridged separate worlds, helping each understand and appreciate the other.

Gertrude Bell (1868–1926) was the daughter of a wealthy English industrialist. She had tremendous ambition, which she used to persuade her parents to give her an education at a time when, for a woman, education was considered secondary to a good marriage. As a result of her intelligence and determination, she won one of the few coveted spots for women at Oxford University. After college, she did not know what to do. Girls of her class usually waited at home for a proposal of marriage. But after Bell returned home, she received an invitation from her uncle to visit Persia (modern-day Iran). Quickly, she set about learning Persian. Later she learned Arabic and begin her own archeological trips into the Syrian deserts.

When World War I broke out, Bell was in the Middle East. Her ability to speak the language, as well as her knowledge of the local tribes and the deserts from her archeological work, caused the British to appoint her to one of the most important jobs in the Desert War, that of Oriental Secretary. The Oriental Secretary was the officer of the embassy who was expected to know about and deal with local affairs, roughly what we call a political officer in an embassy. Bell played a major role in crafting the division of the Middle East into the countries we know today. She also founded the museum in Iraq.

Alexandra David-Néel (1868–1969) was performing in the Paris Opera when she married a banker. As she now had some financial freedom, she decided to act on her lifelong dream to travel to the East. Soon after she married, she sailed alone for India. She assured her husband she be gone only about 18 months; it would be 24 years before she would return home. Upon arriving in India she became intrigued with the Buddhist religion. She felt in order to understand Buddhism, she had first to master Tibetan, the language in which many of the texts were written. In the course of doing so, she plunged so deeply into the culture that she became a Buddhist nun. After several years of study, David-Néel became determined to visit the home of the spiritual leader of the Tibetan Buddhists, the Dalai Lama, who resided in the Holy City of Lhasa, in Tibet. This was quite a challenge because all foreigners were forbidden from entering Lhasa. At the age of 55, she began a long and arduous winter trek across the Himalayas toward Tibet. She succeeded in becoming the first Western woman to visit Lhasa. After returning to France, David-Néel dedicated the rest of her long life to helping Westerners understand the beauty and complexity of Buddhist religion and culture through her many writings.

A wealthy and restless young woman, Annie Montague Alexander (1867–1950) decided to pursue her interests in science and nature rather than live the life of a socialite in San Francisco. She organized numerous expeditions throughout the American West to collect flora, fauna, and fossils. Concerned by the rapid changes occurring due to the growing population, Alexander envisaged a time, all too soon, when much of the natural world of the West would be gone due to urbanization and agricultural development. As a tribute to the land she loved, she decided to create the best natural history museum of the American West. She actually created two museums at the University of California, Berkeley, in which to house the thousands of specimens she had assembled. In the course of her exploration, she discovered new species, seventeen of which are named for her. Though little known, Alexander contributed much to our knowledge of American zoology and paleontology.

Two women in this series are still actively exploring. Sue Hendrickson dropped out of high school and made a living by collecting fish off the Florida Keys to sell to aquariums. An invitation to go on an underwater dive trip changed her life. She became passionate about diving, and soon found herself working with archeologists on wrecks. Hendrickson was often the lead diver, diving first to find out what was there. She realized she had a knack for seeing things others missed. On land, she became an amber collector of pieces of fossilized resin that contained insects and later became a dinosaur hunter. While on a fossil expedition in the Badlands of the Dakotas, Hendrickson discovered the largest *Tyrannosaurus rex* ever found. It has been named Sue in her honor. Depending on the time of year, she can be found diving in the sunken ancient port of Alexandria, Egypt, mapping Spanish wrecks off Cuba's coastline, or in the high, dry lands of ancient forests hunting for dinosaur bones.

Sylvia Earle began her exploration of the sea in the early days of scuba. Smitten with the undersea world, she earned degrees in biology and oceanography. She wanted more than to just study the sea; she wanted to live in the sea. In the early 1970s, Earle was eager to take part in a project in which humans lived in a module underwater for extended periods of time for the U.S. Navy. Unfortunately, when the project was about to begin, she was informed that because she was a woman, she could not go. Undaunted, Earle designed the next phase of the project exclusively for women. This project had far-reaching results. It proved to the U.S. military that women could live well in a confined environment and opened the door for women's entry into the space program.

Earle, ever reaching for new challenges, began designing and testing submersibles, which would allow a human to experience the underwater world more intimately than anything created up to that time. Approaching age 70, her goal is to explore the deepest, darkest place on earth: the 35,800-foot-deep Marianas Trench south of Guam, in the Pacific Ocean.

The experiences of these six women illustrate different paths, different experiences, and different situations, but each led to a similar fulfillment in exploration. All are explorers; all have given us the gift of understanding some aspect of our world. All offer tremendous opportunities to us. Each of us can learn from them and follow in their paths. They are trailblazers; but many trails remain unexplored. There is so much unknown about the world, so much that needs to be understood. For example, less than 5 percent of the ocean has been explored. Thousands of species of plants and animals wait to be discovered. We have not reached every place on earth, and of what we have seen, we often understand very little. Today, we are embarked on the greatest age of exploration. And we go armed with more knowledge than any of the explorers who have gone before us.

What these women teach us is that we need explorers to help us understand what is miraculous in the world around us. The goal for each of us is to find his or her own path and begin the journey.

1

Alone and Unsheltered

The coldness of this land will stop tea from pouring.

—Old Tibetan proverb

It is December 1923, high in the Himalayas. At age 55, this woman has come to Tibet. The lure of faraway places has fascinated her and has driven her to discover what lies beyond her garden gate for more than a half-century. Now, against the will of both the British government and the Dalai Lama, the spiritual head of Tibetan Buddhism, she has made a second trip to Tibet. This time, she intends to fulfill the burning ambition of her life: She is set on becoming the first white woman ever to enter the Forbidden City of Lhasa, capital of Tibet.

Today, the woman and her traveling companion, a young Tibetan lama (monk), have reached the summit of Aigni-la, a lofty mountain pass leading into Tibet's Po *yul* (country). Their latest guide, a local *dokpa* (herdsman), prepares to leave them here. The lama offers him two silver coins for his help. Rather than money, which he would soon spend, the dokpa asks the holy man for a blessing. He prefers to store away merit toward his next lifetime. The lama obliges, and the guide bids them goodbye.

"*Kale pheb* [proceed slowly] lama," he says, "*Kale pheb*, mother!"[1] Having cautioned the lama and the woman to proceed slowly, which is a polite farewell in Tibet, the guide leaves.

The travelers stand alone on the summit, where the snapping of prayer flags marking the top of Aigni-la seems to emphasize their aloneness. They pause only long enough to shout "*Lha gyalo*"[2] ("The gods have won"), the traditional Tibetan exclamation of wayfarers on reaching the summit of mountain passes.

The young lama breathes deeply and stares down the pass. "It will snow,"[3] he says. His tone sounds grave and his mood seems somber, unlike his usual cheerfulness. The woman wonders what vague premonition has momentarily cast a shadow over his customary lighthearted outlook. With a difficult descent facing them, though, she puts aside

Potala Palace looms in the background as a group of Tibetans gather in an outdoor kitchen in Lhasa, the holy capital city of Tibet. Although Lhasa was closed to Westerners, Alexandra David-Néel was an adventurer and devoted Buddhist who was determined to be the first Western woman to enter the Forbidden City.

her troubling thoughts. "Let us be quick,"[4] her friend says, and they start to walk down the hill.

They descend rapidly—the woman a bit *too* rapidly. She loses her footing in the snow and plunges downhill like a human toboggan, using her walking stick to steer. The stocky lama rushes to her side and examines her diminutive five-foot-two-inch frame for injuries. Miraculously, she emerges unscathed from her unintended free fall. The lama comments on the aesthetics of her fall, wryly pointing out the energy-conserving benefits of her unorthodox descent. She accepts his playful gibe without ill will, pleased to see the return of her friend's good humor. They continue on their way.

Snow has already fallen in some places, and the moisture-laden air hints of more to come. As they trudge lower, they find the ground wet and even slightly marshy here and there. Soon they reach the wooded zone, where they find a river springing at the base of Aigni-la. The woman recognizes their discovery as one of the feeder springs of the Tsangpo River. Her map does not show the sources of the Tsangpo, but she knows that it flows west to east, south of Lhasa, and forms the upper course of the mighty Brahmaputra River.

Following the shore of the spring, the two travelers next come upon a large pasture situated at the intersection of three valleys. Moving through one of the valleys, they find another stream. Exhilarated by their second find, the woman suggests ranging off their intended path to search for additional feeder springs. The lama, lacking a similar elation, says, "It will snow, and we have no food."[5]

The woman accepts his words and reflects briefly on their situation and the potential consequences of further exploration. They have three meals left, enough to last them for three days, and only a glance at the upper valleys will satisfy her curiosity. Her decision made, she says, "Forward!"[6]

The snow starts falling softly right after sundown. Against a darkening forest background, the gently falling flakes remind the woman of a scattering of butterflies swirling among the trees, but the fluttering flakes gradually multiply and thicken into a moving veil of whiteness. Her senses tell her that this is "one of those slow snowfalls, whose flakes descend from some inexhaustible heavenly store, shrouding the mighty peaks and burying the valleys." [7]

A few hours later, the steady fall of snow has dampened the exhilaration of fresh discovery. "Let us pitch the tent," the woman says. "We will light a fire inside it and have tea." [8] Using a few stones as weights, they attach one end of their tent to a rock to form a sloping shelter, and then forage for firewood. They finally find enough small branches to boil tea, which suffices as their evening meal. After taking tea, the exhausted travelers sink quickly into a deep sleep. The silent snow continues to fall.

In her dreams, the woman holds back a great weight that is trying to crush her. She wakens with a start to find that their tent has collapsed under a heavy accumulation of snow and threatens to smother them. Working together, the occupants manage to break free to the surface before the weight of the accumulating snow makes escape impossible. Rather than risk a similar occurrence, they tramp through the snow for the rest of the night.

Shortly after noon the next day, the weary travelers chance upon a *sa phug* (earthen cave). Rejoicing at this stroke of luck, they take refuge in the warmth of the cave's dry interior. They soften the rumblings of their deprived stomachs with a little *tsampa* (barley gruel) and relieve their thirst by melting snow in their mouths. The snow shows no sign of letting up, so the exhausted wayfarers turn in and sleep straight through until the following dawn. They awake to find the snow still falling, as it has for more than 40 hours.

The woman decides to make one more exploratory trek

into a gorge higher up in search of another feeder stream. She leads the ascent. Her companion trails behind reluctantly. Seeking a shortcut, the lama slips and crashes into a shallow ravine. He cries out in pain. His partner backtracks quickly and finds him lying on the white, bloodstained snow. She helps him to his feet, but his foot will not support his weight.

"I will try to carry you," she tells him. "We must go back to the sa phug, and there we will think over the matter."[9] Unfortunately, she lacks the strength to haul him through the deep snow and treacherous footing, so they spend the next several hours crawling back to the cave together. Again, they sleep until dawn.

At first light, the woman awakes to find her friend trying to walk with the aid of his staff, but he cannot. Outside, the snow still billows down without letup. Their situation has become desperate. Despite the always-present danger of prowling wolves, bears, or leopards, she decides to leave the lama alone while she sets out in search of help from a camp of nomadic dokpas.

She lurches out into the seemingly ceaseless snowfall and follows the valley down as far as she can, tramping for hours on end and finding only two deserted dokpa camps. The shadows lengthen and darken around her, and the imminence of night forces her to turn back toward the sa phug. She has failed to find help, but she can at least return to the cave bearing some cow dung for a warming fire. Removing her upper dress, she gathers a night's supply of cow chips from one of the dokpa camps and uses her dress as a satchel.

She starts to retrace her steps, head bent against the whirling snow. Her thin Chinese underdress soon proves inadequate. In minutes, she feels as if she is immersed in an icy bath. Worse, she suddenly realizes that she has lost all sense of the cave's location. Has she tramped too high up the valley? Does the sa phug still lie below her? The night has now wrapped her in total blackness, and she cannot see a thing in any direction. The implications of the woman's predicament leave little to her imagination.

At age 55, Alexandra David-Néel is alone and unsheltered in the Himalayas, in the middle of a blizzard that shows no sign of stopping.

2

Silent Calls

Ever since I was five years old, a tiny precocious child of
Paris, I wished to move out of the narrow limits in which, like
all children of my age, I was then kept. I craved to go beyond
the garden gate, to follow the road that passed it by, and to
set out for the unknown.

—Alexandra David-Néel

Two years after her birth on October 24, 1868, in the comfortable Parisian suburb of Saint Mandé, Alexandra David escaped the confines of a controlled existence for the first time. She slipped out the door of her grandparents' house and set out to see how far the road in front of their garden would lead her. Fortunately for the adventurous little tot, her parents caught up with her and brought her home safely. The incident marked the start of her lifelong fascination with travel and the lure of faraway places.

The hours of her childhood bear witness to a series of unauthorized explorations. At the age of five, while visiting the Bois de Vincennes, near Paris, with her governess, she again slipped the bonds of adult supervision to explore the forest on her own. At length, a *gendarme* (policeman) found the little girl and escorted her to the local police station. An angry governess soon arrived to claim the missing tyke and demanded, "Alexandra, where have you been?" [10]

The child replied, "I was exploring the *bois*, [woods] searching for my very own tree." [11] In the tone of her voice, her answer implied that her latest escapade was nothing extraordinary for a child of five on a pleasant spring excursion. She in fact resented having her exploration cut short and vowed revenge on adults who interfered with the rightful pursuits of children. Someday, she promised herself, she would journey far beyond the horizon and not allow anyone to stop her. She would give the whole world reason to ask, "Alexandra, where have you been?"

No one can say for certain how many times the irrepressible Alexandra ran off on some adventurous flight as a child, but such occasions ran high in number. "Adventure," she would say later, "is my only reason for living." [12] Clearly, wanderlust, a strong urge to travel, possessed her at a very early age. The source of her compulsion is open to question. Much of her motivation probably stemmed from a pressing desire to escape

9

the ambiance of a home overshadowed by the apparently loveless marriage of her parents.

Her father, Louis Pierre David, was born on July 6, 1815, in Tours, France. Although he was a Huguenot, a French Protestant, the family name has Jewish roots. Alexandra liked to hint that her family had belonged to the Albigensians, a heretical sect that existed during the Middle Ages, and thus had suffered religious persecution.

Alexandra's mother, Alexandrine Borghmans, was of mixed Dutch, Norwegian, and Siberian ancestry. She was a devout Catholic. Because of her Siberian lineage, Alexandra, the future explorer of Central Asia, often proudly claimed to be part Mongol. According to Barbara Foster and Michael Foster, authors of Alexandra's definitive biography, her claim of Mongol heritage "was the only positive thing she ever said about her mother." [13]

Louis reached maturity during the reign of Louis Philippe, the Citizen King, enthroned by the July Revolution of 1830. Slender, earnest, and quite good-looking, he entered the working world as a schoolteacher, his father's profession, but later became a journalist and a political activist. His liberal activism eventually led to his exile in Louvain, Belgium, when Louis Bonaparte proclaimed himself Napoleon III, staged a coup against Louis Philippe, and installed himself as emperor of France in 1852. In Louvain, Louis met Alexandrine, the 22-year-old adopted daughter of the mayor, and asked for her hand in marriage. After a simple ceremony in 1854, the couple entered into a marriage in which both, according to Alexandra, "were unhappy from the start." [14]

The differences of Alexandra's parents-to-be far exceeded their similarities. Louis did not want children. Alexandrine longed to bear a son who would rise to high station in her beloved Catholic Church. After 14 years of a childless and steadily souring union, Alexandrine, at the age of 36, informed her husband that she was pregnant. Louis reacted to the news by insisting on taking advantage of an amnesty for all political exiles and returning to France. He wanted his child to be able to claim French citizenship.

In 1868, the Davids moved to Saint Mandé. Alexandrine spent the months of her pregnancy in a bed of multiple pillows and silk sheets, reading the American adventure novels of James Fenimore Cooper and appeasing her appetite with chocolates. In October, she bore a daughter rather than a hoped-for son. The new mother threw herself into a mound of lace-trimmed pillows and sobbed mightily to vent her disappointment.

Three days later, the girl was baptized Louise Eugénie Alexandrine Marie David. Later, the child asked to be called Alexandra, and her family honored her request. Alexandrine had not wanted a girl and made no secret of it. Abdicating her responsibility as a mother, she turned the girl's care over to a succession of nurses and governesses. In later years, her daughter would never forgive her. A sense of being unwanted in her own home no doubt contributed greatly to Alexandra's persistent urges to leave.

In 1873, Alexandrine finally gave birth to a boy, but her hopes of raising a future Catholic bishop ended forever when her fragile son died only six months later. In her grief, Madame David pressured her husband to return to Belgium. Louis finally relented in 1874, but not before having Alexandra rebaptized in secret, this time as a Protestant. Although Alexandra came to identify with the independent spirit and social conscience of the Huguenots, she failed to find solace in their austere services in time of need.

After converting to Protestantism, Alexandra developed an interest in comparative religions by the age of six. While living in the suburbs of the Belgian capital of Brussels, she fell in love with books, both as sources of knowledge and avenues of escape from a depressing home atmosphere. For pure escape reading, she favored the fantasies of Jules Verne and often imagined herself exceeding the daring exploits of his heroes. Bored with the childhood games of her peers, she cultivated an interest in music and soon became an accomplished pianist. The melodies of Mozart, Schubert, and Schumann afforded her still another means of escaping the drabness of her daily life.

Escape became Alexandra's passion, and she begrudged each hour and each day of her youth that was lost to humdrum activities. "I cried bitter tears more than once, having the profound feeling that life was going by, that the days of my youth were going by, empty, without interest, without joy," she wrote years later. "I understood that I was wasting time that would never return, that I was losing hours that could have been beautiful." [15]

While attending a Calvinist boarding school at the age of ten, Alexandra became depressed and starting losing weight at an alarming rate. Acting on the advice of the family doctor, her mother enrolled her in a Catholic school at the nearby convent of Bois Fleuri. Alexandra blossomed physically and mentally at Bois Fleuri. On six meals a day, she regained her lost weight and even a little more than she needed. She continued to pursue her interests in comparative theologies, cutting her intellectual teeth on the written delicacies of religious and social thinkers such as Augustine, Kierkegaard, and Proudhon.

At 13, Alexandra grew enraptured by a tale about Buddha, an earlier incarnation of Siddhartha Gautama, who was the founder of the Buddhist religion. The Buddhists believe in rebirth, a succession of lives leading to *nirvana,* a state of blissful void. Buddha, as the story goes, met a tiger in the jungle and sacrificed his own flesh to feed her starving cubs. His singular act of compassion touched her deeply and started her down the religious path known to Buddhists as the "middle way," which is basically a course midway between extremes.

Although leaning toward Buddhism, Alexandra held her options open. In her bedroom, she kept a Chinese porcelain Buddha with a light burning constantly before it. Above her bed, she hung a crucifix, and a large Bible occupied a privileged place on her table. Every night she read several verses from the Bible before retiring. She adopted a favorite phrase from Ecclesiastes as a creed to live by: "Walk in the ways of thine heart and in sight of thine eyes."[16] She held true to her creed through successive phases of social radicalism, bohemianism, and Buddhism.

As she matured, her interests continued to broaden. By the age of 15, she had begun to study music and voice privately. She would later use her training professionally to support herself. Over her long and eventful life, Alexandra would repeatedly recall happy memories of her years at Bois Fleuri. "It was for her a period of true awakening," wrote Ruth Middleton, one of her biographers, "when she was free to extend her curiosity in all directions."[17] One extension of her curiosity led her into the occult (the supernatural, mystical, or magical) world of London at age 15.

In response to Alexandra's request, a mysterious English occultist named Elisabeth Morgan sent her a journal published by the Society of the Supreme Gnosis. Gnosis is the esoteric knowledge of spiritual truth held by the ancient Gnostics to be essential for salvation. The journal contained an array of cryptic thought, symbology, and language, including scraps of Sanskrit, one of the oldest known Indo-European languages, which both perplexed and intrigued her. Alexandra decided to seek answers to her questions in person. In her fifteenth summer, while the Davids vacationed at the seaside city of Ostend, Belgium, Alexandra hiked into Holland and crossed the English Channel. She found Elisabeth Morgan but little else. The older woman quickly persuaded the adventuresome adolescent to return home.

In 1885, Alexandra, without a word to anyone, traveled by train to Switzerland. At the Swiss frontier, carrying little more than an umbrella and the maxims of Epictetus, a Greek philosopher, she hiked alone through the Alps, via Saint

Gotthard Pass into the Italian lake country. This time, however, circumstances forced her to suppress her pride and wire home for help: "Come get me. [I] am without money." [18] Alexandrine met the illicit traveler in Milan, and mother and daughter returned to Brussels by train.

Soon after her latest unsanctioned excursion, Alexandra set out again for distant destinations. This time, she toured Spain on a heavy, fixed-pinion bicycle, carrying her belongings on the handlebars. When she returned to Brussels, her mother put her to work managing one of her fabric concessions. Alexandrine hoped to put an end to Alexandra's itinerant behavior, but Alexandra neither liked nor was much good at merchandizing.

Alexandra escaped the marketplace and her mother's dominance by entering the Royal Conservatory in April 1886, where she advanced her musical talents and cultivated her soprano voice. Two years later, a letter from Elisabeth Morgan offered her a chance to engage in the then-fashionable study of mysticism and to board cheaply at the Supreme Gnosis. Alexandra leaped at the opportunity to expand her knowledge, especially because it meant escaping, however temporarily, her mother's control.

At London's Victoria Station, a member of the secret gnostic society met the 20-year-old mademoiselle and escorted her to the Society's home. The vice president greeted her in a flowing robe with long sleeves, adorned with several brooches and medals symbolizing her office, and provided Alexandra with a comfortable room of her own, as well as an introduction to the other society members.

Alexandra enjoyed her stay in London. She was delighted to find herself among friendly people with similar interests. The other members treated her with discretion, and they did not try to impose their beliefs on her. They left her free to improve her English and to study the arcane subjects of her own choosing. "She spent long hours in the library, which contained a large collection of translations of Chinese and Indian texts and other esoteric subjects such as metaphysics, philosophy, astrology, and alchemy," wrote Ruth Middleton. "She discovered the infinite riches of the British Museum."[19] Alexandra also discovered romance and feminism.

The awakening mademoiselle became attracted to a slender, delicately featured, young French artist named Jacques Villemain who also lived at the "Gnose." Few details of their covert liaison exist, but one mystical moment in their relationship has endured. It involves Villemain's belief in astral figures (doubles in a counterworld of nonmaterial reality) and one of his paintings depicting a snowcapped peak looming over a bleak salt lake. While examining the surreal scene, Alexandra reached out to touch it and Villemain snatched it away from her, warning her that she was about to enter the painting. He never explained to her satisfaction precisely what he had meant by "entering into a painting."[20] Decades later, while entering a Tibetan plain rimmed by snowcapped peaks, Alexandra experienced an episode of déjà vu and thought immediately of Villemain's eerie landscape.

While Alexandra sojourned in London, Elisabeth Morgan, whom she saw now and then and would later refer to as her "godmother," introduced her to other members of London's burgeoning occult society. Among them was Madame Helena Petrovna Blavatsky, a cofounder of the Theosophical Society in New York in 1875. Madame Blavatsky, a spiritualist and writer, claimed to have direct telepathic contact with Tibetan monks and their esoteric teachings. She passed on their teachings through her society and in her books, which included *The Secret Doctrine* and *The Key to Theosophy*.

While attending sessions at the Theosophical Society, Alexandra struck up a friendship with Annie Besant. Annie, a strong-willed woman much like Alexandra, was an outspoken advocate of women's rights and interests. Her feminist activism came at a time soon after the French writer Honoré de Balzac had defined the role of eighteenth-century women in this way: "The destiny of woman and her sole glory are to make beat the hearts of men."[21]

THEOSOPHY

Theosophy is a religious philosophy with mystical elements. It dates back to the ancient age. The word *theosophy* derives from the Greek *theos* (god) and *sophia* (wisdom) and generally translates as "divine wisdom."

Theosophy comprises a religious or semireligious set of occult beliefs that reject Judeo-Christian revelation and theology (religious doctrine). It incorporates components of Buddhism, Hinduism, and other religions, particularly a belief in reincarnation. Theosophists claim a mystic insight into the nature of God and the laws of the universe. They hold that the truest knowledge comes not through reason or the senses but through a direct communion of the soul with divine reality.

Theosophical convictions appear in gnosticism, Neoplatonism, and other ancient religious and philosophical movements. History credits German mystic Jakob Böhme (1575–1624) with being the father of theosophy. In modern times, theosophy is usually linked to the teachings of the Theosophical Society. The society originated in New York City in 1875. Its founders include American attorney Henry Steel Olcutt, Russian spiritualist Helena Patrovna Blavatsky, and others. In 1889, British feminist and social reformer Annie Wood Besant joined the society and served as its international president from 1907 until her death in 1933.

The principal aims of the Theosophical Society are first, to establish a nucleus of the universal brotherhood of humankind, without distinction of race, creed, sex, class, or color; second, to advance the study of comparative religion, philosophy, and science; and third, to explore unexplained laws of nature and the untapped powers of human beings.

Alexandra and Annie saw their roles quite differently. Both women figuratively thumbed their noses at Balzac's belittling assessment of women and went on to prove him wrong: Annie ascended to the presidency of the Theosophical Society after the death of Madame Blavatsky in 1891 and Alexandra earned world acclaim as the explorer of Tibet and its arcane practices.

In 1889, Alexandra concluded that London had served its purpose in broadening her mystical horizons. She always seemed to know the right time to move on to her next destination on the road of life. When she told Annie of her plans to resume her studies of comparative religions in Paris, her friend arranged accommodations for her at the Paris branch of the Theosophical Society in the Latin Quarter.

The city of her birth offered many opportunities for Alexandra's continuing search for knowledge and meaning in her life. She enrolled at the Collège de France, studied Sanskrit under the esteemed Professor Philippe-Edward Foucaux, and attended classes in Oriental languages at the Sorbonne. Paris held many wonders for her, and she managed to visit most of them. She replaced London's British Museum with the Musée Guimet, a museum featuring Far Eastern art and religious objects.

At the Guimet, under the beneficent stare of a gilt statue of Buddha, Alexandra "spent long hours in the library, listening to the silent calls of the pages" that she leafed through. "Vocations are born," she wrote later, adding, "mine was born there." [22] In Paris, she began a serious study of Buddhism, a spiritual calling that she would answer for the rest of her long life.

3

The Universal Law

I belong to a new breed. We are few in number but we will accomplish our mission. I am doing what I must.

—Alexandra David-Néel

One evening in 1889, Alexandra stayed late at the Musée
Guimet, poring over translations of sacred texts in the library.
By then, she had become enamored of the huge Japanese
statue of Buddha that was installed in a niche overlooking
her place of study. Impelled by its presence, and thinking
herself alone, she joined her palms together in Oriental
fashion and bowed to the gilt image. Suddenly, a woman's
voice emanated from the shadows: "May the blessings of the
Buddha be with you, mademoiselle."[23] The voice, friendly but
amused, belonged to the Comtesse de Bréant, a prominent
student of Oriental philosophy who often spent long hours
at the museum.

"This very beautiful Japanese statue made me think of
the great sage it is intended to resemble," Alexandra replied,
"and I salute the doctrine it represents."[24] In moments, the
two women discovered much in common and entered into
an instant friendship. During the ensuing weeks, the
comtesse introduced Alexandra to the Parisian occult scene,
just as Elisabeth Morgan had shown her around similar
environs in London. The two new friends attended numerous
lectures at the Pythagorean Society, a cultural foundation
where Alexandra met many of the city's leading occultists
and orientalists. In the evenings, they sought diversions
in the cafés or salons and at the opera, savoring such
performances as *Thaïs, Aïda,* and *Madam Butterfly,* all
of which featured Eastern settings and portrayed women
as victims.

In addition to Far Eastern religions, Alexandra, baptized
first as a Catholic, then again as a Protestant, showed a keen
interest in the ideas of Plato and in the sacred scriptures of the
Qu'ran (Koran). She did not surrender herself to the tenets
of Buddhism without first exposing her mind and spirit to a
variety of religious and philosophical alternatives, including
Hinduism. At the same time, free spirit that she was, Alexandra
flirted with every radical political thought of the day, no doubt

encouraged by her father's Far-Left activism and through her association with Elisée Reclus.

Reclus was Louis David's friend; neighbor in Ixelles, Belgium; and fellow Leftist. He regularly opened his attractive home and garden to groups of young people seeking to explore and discuss controversial concepts. "It was under his roof," wrote Barbara Foster and Michael Foster, "that Alexandra met political exiles, bearded freethinkers, and other merchants of dreams."[25] Quite possibly it was while under his activist sway that Alexandra ran into trouble with the Belgian police.

Jeanne Denys, another of Alexandra's biographers, insisted that Alexandra "must have had a run-in with the law." Upon her inquiry, the Belgian police told Denys, "There exists [on Alexandra] dossier number 508–533 at the Foreign Police of the Ministry of Justice."[26] The contents of the dossier will likely never become public because such files are open only to government officials or relatives. Regardless of its contents, which probably do not include reprehensible crimes, the mere existence of the dossier would later cast a shadow on Alexandra's past.

At this time, Alexandra suffered her first attack of neurasthenia, an emotional and psychological disorder. It is characterized by lack of motivation, feelings of inadequacy, and psychosomatic symptoms. Today, the disorder is called "depression," an equally vague term. She would struggle with the recurring malady throughout her life.

Perhaps more than anything else during this period of rebelling and awakening, Alexandra enjoyed listening to the Comtesse de Bréant describe her travels in Asia. Her aristocratic patron's tales of the Indian subcontinent filled the young woman with wondrous visions of exotic places: Alexandra had long dreamed of sailing to India. Then, suddenly, Elisabeth Morgan, Alexandra's "godmother," died in 1891 and left her a small inheritance. Alexandra's mother wanted her to invest the money in a nice tobacconist shop, but the young rebel held other ideas: The small but tidy sum would pay nicely for a passage to India. At age 23, she set sail for Ceylon, which is now Sri Lanka.

Steaming through the Red Sea on her outward passage to India, the suffocating heat quickly introduced Alexandra to the differences between far-off places as imagined and as they really are. She embarked on her first journey to Asia expecting to find a land filled with flowers and spices, verdant forests, azure skies, and *saddhus* (holy men) contemplating past and future lives under the leafy branches of banyan trees. Instead, she found dirt and dust, driving monsoon rains, teeming crowds, splendor amid squalor, and a crushing heat most of the time. Despite her shattered preconceptions of India, she readily exchanged her imagined views for the realities of the East and delighted in the trade-off.

Following a 15-day voyage, Alexandra arrived in Colombo, the capital of Ceylon. She checked into the nearest hotel, changed her clothes, and set out for the closest Buddhist temple. Her attire, which the Comtesse de Bréant had helped her select, consisted of an immaculate white dress with long sleeves, white gloves, a broad-brimmed hat, and the indispensable parasol to shield the fair Frenchwoman from the tropical sun. Traveling by *pousse-pousse* (rickshaw), she arrived at the temple in good time, where she experienced the first genuine disappointment of her trip: A larger-than-life-size statue of the Buddha that was painted a shocking canary yellow, a far cry from the exquisite gilt image of the Buddha at the Musée Guimet.

The next day, hoping to find a more appealing image of the Buddha, Alexandra visited the temple complex at Kelinaya, several miles outside Colombo. She found a large temple at the center of an impressive array of buildings. Inside the temple, she found, to her dismay, another canary-yellow statue of the

Buddha. Clearly, the East Indian conception of the Buddha differed greatly from the Oriental images to which she had become accustomed. Alexandra cut short her stay in Ceylon and boarded a boat "the size of a nutshell"[27] to cross the Bay of Tuticorin for India, consoling herself that her trip had only just begun.

The little craft crossed the short distance to the Indian subcontinent in rough seas. It shuddered, moaned, and threatened to capsize. Rats poured out of the bilge and into the passenger cabins, along with giant cockroaches, spiders, lice, and other odious vermin seeking safer traveling accommodations. Alexandra succumbed to seasickness. She soon found herself covered from head to toe with skittering insects and was too weak to brush them aside. Deck passengers in danger of being swept overboard by crashing waves shrieked in fear for their lives. Despite the unpleasantness, the little boat deposited its passengers safely, if slightly shaken, in Tuticorin.

The rest of Alexandra's first trip to India proved much more pleasant. Traveling by train, she ranged from almost the southern tip of the subcontinent to as far north as the foothills of Mount Kanchenjunga, whose five snow-covered peaks rise majestically along the Nepali-Sikkimese frontier. Alexandra formally joined the Theosophical Society while she was in Adyar, which is near Madras, the main port on India's southeast coast. The Society's international headquarters is located in Adyar. For a time, she studied Sanskrit with the Theosophists. She then followed the standard tourist itinerary north to Benares, now known as Varanasi, a holy city on the banks of the sacred Ganges River 400 miles west-northwest of Calcutta.

At Benares, Swami Bashkarananda, impressed with Alexandra's knowledge of Hinduism, invited her to study yoga under him. The swami lived year round in a rose garden and imparted his deep understanding of Indian thought to a small group of devoted followers. Alexandra eagerly accepted his invitation.

At age 25, Alexandra was preparing to become initiated as a *sannyasin* (renunciate), a person who leads a life of contemplation and strict self-denial for religious purposes, but when her money ran out, she was forced to return to Brussels. As she left, the swami whispered in her ear: "Impermanence is the universal law." [28] His words suited the young woman's itinerant existence like a sail billowing to a following wind.

Back in Brussels, necessity again forced Alexandra to rely on the generosity of her parents for subsistence, but she knew that the time had come to assume responsibility for her own support. She resumed her musical studies, first in the Conservatory of Brussels and later in the Paris Conservatoire, where she completed her studies and won awards for her honeyed coloratura voice (a light, agile soprano specializing in elaborate vocalizations). Beyond the kudos of her peers, her greatest award came when her mother said, "I salute you, great artist." [29]

During her days at the conservatories, Alexandra also found time to express her rebellious worldview. Encouraged by Elisée Reclus, she began to write *Pour La Vie (For Life)*, a radical political treatise condemning anything that might possibly infringe on individual rights. In a foreword to the book, Reclus wrote, "This is a proud book, written by a woman prouder still." [30] Reclus published the book himself five years later, but Alexandra profited little from its limited printing. Becoming a published author, she learned, carried no guarantee of rich rewards.

In 1894, Alexandra spent weeks making the rounds of Parisian musical directors. As an aspiring chanteuse (concert or nightclub singer), she was starting late. The life of a soprano is short, and she felt an added eagerness to get started in her career. In one audition after another, she sang before directors with indifferent ears, rendering the works of such renowned composers as Bizet, Gounod, Puccini, and particularly Jules Massenet.

At last, in the autumn of 1895, Alexandra landed a well-paying position as the *première cantatrice* (first-ranking singer) with the road company of *L'Opéra-Comique.* In addition to good wages and premier status, her new position allowed her to return to the Orient at company expense. She again put to sea on a steamer bound for "somewhere east of Suez." [31] She spent the next two years touring French Indochina, now Vietnam, appearing in Hanoi, Haiphong, and elsewhere, while performing lead roles in such operas as *La Traviata* and *Carmen.* The now-seasoned professional returned to Paris in 1897.

Alexandra had hoped from the start of her singing career to become a prima donna (first lady, or principal singer) with the Opéra de Paris. Upon her return to Paris however, she received only an offer to perform in a bit part at far less money than she had received in the Orient. She turned down the demeaning offer and instead embarked on a tour of the Midi (the south of France) in the spring of 1897. The tour reduced the travel that she loved so much to short trips between cities in the provinces.

While Alexandra performed in the southern provinces for the next two-plus years, she maintained a permanent residence in Paris. One evening early in this period, while attending a meeting of the Theosophical Society, she met a fair-haired young composer with a beard named Jean Haustont. In this tall, slender composer, she found a fellow orientalist with similar interests in music. Although she was now approaching the age of 30, she felt no compulsion to marry, but her economic status inclined her toward acquiring a roommate to share the rent. Soon after their meeting, the couple established a joint residency at 3 rue Nicolo, in suburban Passy, as Monsieur and Madame Myrial. Alexandra

THE ROLES SHE PLAYED

As an aspiring opera star singing under the stage name of Alexandra Myrial, Alexandra David empathized totally with the characters she played. Her ability to understand and identify with the feelings, thoughts, and experiences of others enabled her to project the hopes and fears, wants and needs, and the range of human emotions of those she portrayed on stage.

Alexandra's first operatic triumph came in the role of "Violetta" in Italian composer Guiseppe Verdi's *La Traviata,* the story of a young man's love for a dying courtesan, adapted from Alexandre Dumas's *La Dame aux camélias* (*The Lady of the Camellias*). In Léo Delibes's *Lakmé*, an opera containing Oriental scenes orchestrated with music of an innovative, exotic nature, David excelled in the title role. For her delicate renditions of Delibes's coloratura aria "Bell Song," she garnered many well-deserved accolades.

The role with which Alexandra most identified combined the talents of two of her favorites. She sang the title role in Jules Massenet's opera *Thaïs,* based on Anatole France's novel of the same name. It tells a story of a courtesan in Egypt who redeems herself and becomes a saint. In *Manon*, another of Masennet's operas, this one based on *Manon Lescaut*, a seven-volume novel by Antoine François Prévost, Alexandra again played a courtesan. This story recounts the fall of a young man of good family who ruins his life for a trollop.

While on tour in French Indochina (Vietnam), Alexandra sang the title role in Georges Bizet's *Carmen* for several nights running. *Carmen* tells the tragic tale of a perfidious gypsy girl and a young Spanish officer of the guard. The title role calls for a mezzo-soprano, a huskier voice than a coloratura that ranges between a soprano and a contralto. In performing the role, Alexandra overtaxed her more delicate coloratura voice and sent it into decline, substantially shortening her operatic career.

chose the false name from a character in Victor Hugo's novel *Les Miserables*. The acclaimed Hugo was one of Louis David's best friends and had played with Alexandra when she was a child. She would use the pseudonym as a pen name for some of her early writings.

While sharing their lives and quarters at rue Nicolo, the couple collaborated on a one-act lyric drama entitled *Lidia*. Haustont composed the music; Alexandra wrote the words. They could find no one to stage the play, and it faded into theatrical obscurity. Alexandra, still mildly fascinated with her Bohemian lifestyle, continued to write and produced an autobiographical novel that she named *Le Grand Art: journal d'une actrice (High Art: Memoirs of an Actress)*. In the book, she revealed the social and moral values of theater life. She also disclosed much of her personal struggle to come to grips with her awakening sensuality. Alexandra attempted and failed to have *High Art* published several years later; therefore, her autobiographical indiscretions were never subjected to public scrutiny.

By the end of the century, Alexandra had begun to tire of her Parisian companion and *la vie de boheme*, the bohemian life. The ever-restless wanderer still held visions of the five snow-capped peaks of Kanchenjunga, which she had seen from India's northern frontier, and she could not forget the "captivating Tibetan music"[32] that echoed hauntingly in that high country. Someday, she vowed, she would return to India.

In the meantime, an opportunity to sing at the Opera of Athens arose in the autumn of 1899. Alexandra accepted the engagement without a second thought. Traveling halfway to the Orient no doubt seemed better to her than not traveling at all. She corresponded with Haustont for a time, but he eventually went to China to teach music. He spent the rest of his days in the Far East, and Alexandra would never try to find him there.

In the summer of 1900, after her commitment in Athens had expired, Alexandra received an invitation to perform with the municipal opera in Tunis, Tunisia, in North Africa. Her voice had begun to falter and become unreliable, and she now recognized that her days as a self-sustaining chanteuse were limited. If she worried at all about losing her means of support, her concern was needless. At the age of 32, her life was about to undergo a dramatic change. Impermanence, after all, is the universal law.

4

"On the Threshold of Nirvana"

Adieu, dearest Nini. Your mother and your father send their wishes for happiness and their congratulations on the threshold of the new and brilliant life that opens to you.

—Louis David, in a letter to his daughter Alexandra

During the last decade of the nineteenth century, as an adjunct to her downward-spiraling musical career, Alexandra David had begun to publish essays on a broad range of topics, including politics, women's rights, and Buddhism. Although her writing was attracting interest in Paris and Brussels, the male-dominated literary scene of the time rarely took seriously the work of an unmarried woman. "The presence of a husband was required for entry into the 'serious' world of arts and letters," wrote biographer Ruth Middleton. She further observed, "For women at this time, even those with independent means, the options remained those open to them for centuries: marriage, the church, or caring for elderly parents."[33] At the age of 32, marriage may well have been the last thing on David's mind, but things do have a way of changing.

In September 1900, after appearing with the municipal opera in Tunis, David accepted the musical directorship of the casino of Tunis. Keenly conscious of her weakening vocal cords, she felt delighted to remain gainfully employed in the profession she so loved. Evenings found her at the piano in the casino, a gathering place for lonely Frenchmen in the colony. She entertained her patrons, mostly men, with light arias and café ballads and charmed them with the mystique of a well-traveled Parisian chanteuse. It was here that Philippe Néel entered her life.

Néel, born in Alès, in the south of France, had an ancient Norman lineage. He had been afforded a fine education in engineering, and he had followed his profession to North Africa. He had risen to the position of chief engineering officer with the French railroad company *Chemin de Fer d'Afrique du Nord* (North African Railway) after his important work in constructing the railway from Bône, Algeria, to Guelma, Tunisia.

Still a bachelor at age 39, with sharp features, clear blue eyes, and a jaunty mustache, Néel appeared to have the world right where he wanted it. He sported a lavish wardrobe that featured frock coats and high collars with cravat and stickpin, and he owned a villa on the Mediterranean, and a yacht named *l'Hirondelle* (the *Swallow*). Free as a swallow, Néel flitted from one romantic tryst to another, but as he neared the fortieth year of his bachelor life, what Néel wanted most was a wife and children.

When Néel met Alexandra David, he recognized in her a quality that at once set her apart from the long succession of women in his life. At the same time, David must have felt strongly attracted to Néel. On September 15, soon after meeting him in the casino, she accepted his invitation to join him on the *Swallow*. This seems to suggest that she shared his thoughts about marriage and children, but she did not. She felt no urge to trade her freedom for the bonds of matrimony, but their friendship grew and eventually it would blossom.

She continued to write for the radical magazines and sometimes journeyed to Paris and Brussels to stay in touch with her editors. A sampling of her radicalism can be found in an article she wrote entitled "The Origins of Myths and Their Influence on Social Justice," in which she lashed out at the Judeo-Christian tradition and characterized its priests as descendants of witch doctors. In contrast, Buddhism, in her view, was both rational and liberal. "She hoped for a revolution of thought and sentiment," wrote biographers Barbara Foster and Michael Foster, "not for the masses but to free the individual."[34]

In 1902, David, possibly with the help of Néel's influence, upgraded her station at the casino to the position of artistic director. Néel continued to vie for her affection and she continued to give him hope while holding his marital aspirations in check. That year, she accompanied an expedition of German botanists into the southern desert. While the botanists searched for flora, she cultivated her interest in the Bedouins (Arabic-speaking desert nomads). In Tunis, David enjoyed hearing the muezzin (crier) call faithful Muslims to prayer, and she delighted in studying the Koran (the sacred book of

Muslims.) By the end of the year, she had also advanced her writing with two articles in the influential *Mercure de France*. One of the articles focused on "The Tibetan Clergy and Its Doctrines," a precursor of things to come.

In early 1904, Néel wrote to Louis David, seeking to fulfill the time-honored tradition of a suitor. Alexandra's father responded with surprise, writing, in part:

> Your letter caused me great astonishment. Until today my daughter had shown such a firm determination never to forgo her liberty, and had constantly protested against the inferior state that the law imposes on a woman in all the acts of her life after marriage. Your letter today has led me to believe that Alexandra has strongly modified her ideas, and if this is so Monsieur, I see no reason to refuse my consent to an honorable union.[35]

Alexandra's aging father was nearing his ninetieth year and had posted fair warning of his daughter's free-spirited ways to Monsieur Néel. The rest he left to him.

On August 4, 1904, Alexandra David and Philippe Néel exchanged nuptial vows in a civil ceremony. At the age of 36, David had finally yielded to Néel's tenacity. In her journal entry for the day, she noted indelicately, "I married that horrible *Alouch* at the French consulate in Tunis."[36] Her notation implies a hint of resentment at having allowed Néel to cajole her into marriage, yet her affection for her persistent suitor showed in the pet name that she chose for him. *Alouche,* meaning "sheep" in Arabic, was a nickname suggested to her by his curly hair. She would call him "Mouchy" for the rest of their married life.

The newlyweds sailed for France and honeymooned in the spa town of Plombiers. After taking the waters for a week, Néel returned to Tunis and David-Néel went to Paris to make the rounds of potential publishers. While in Paris, she received news that her father was gravely ill and left at once for Brussels. She found her father dying and her mother ill, alternating between hysteria and helplessness. David-Néel watched over her beloved father's last days, feeling distraught and depressed and finding solace only in the letters of her dear and understanding Mouchy. After several weeks, her ordeal ended.

"My father was buried at Ucele [Uccle, a suburb of Brussels]," David-Néel wrote later. "He was placed in his coffin at 10 A.M. I left the house at 7 P.M. and installed myself *chez* [in the house or home of] Elisée Reclus." [37] For the first time in her life, she had been forced to cope with the death of someone whom she truly loved. Through it all, Mouchy's letters provided her with tender comfort and solid support.

In the winter of 1904, David-Néel returned to Tunis and moved into Néel's charming Moorish-style villa on the Mediterranean. Néel had named it *La Goulette* (The Waterwheel). Complete with whitewashed walls, arcades, arches, a cool patio, and dancing fountains, La Goulette provided David-Néel with safe haven from the world. The next year, while redecorating the villa, she learned of the death of her mentor, Elisée Reclus.

Crushed, she worked through her grief, writing for the journals and lecturing in the great cities of Europe. Her subjects, always controversial, included Buddhism, Zionism (advocating the establishment of a Jewish state) in Palestine, and radical feminism. Her travels over the next seven years, whether by design or otherwise, kept her apart from her husband for much of the time. Her marriage began to unravel. During this period, she suffered recurring attacks of neurasthenia, perhaps induced or aggravated by feelings of guilt over her failure to take an active role in her marriage. Nevertheless, she continued to travel, and seemed either unwilling or incapable of an active role in the marriage she had once described as a "heart-rending comedy." [38]

In 1910, she lectured before the London Buddhist Society

and continued her lectures on Buddhism in Edinburgh and in Brussels. Her preoccupation with Buddhism began to occupy more and more of her life and work. While on the road,

BUDDHISM

Buddhism, the religion of about one-eighth of the world's people, originated 2,500 years ago in northern India. It derives from the teachings of Buddha, regarded by his followers as one of a continuing series of enlightened beings. In the Indian Sanskrit language, *Budh* means "to wake up, to know"; thus, *Buddha* means "the awakened or enlightened one."

Legend holds that Siddhartha Gautama rejected his indulgent lifestyle as a young man and embarked upon a life's course of rigorous self-denial. One day, while meditating under a Bo (short for *Bodhi*, or "enlightenment") tree, he felt close to reaching the truth. He sat quietly under the tree for 49 days, resisting the temptations of evil demons, until he attained the bliss and knowledge he had been seeking. His place of meditation became known as the "immovable spot." Gautama spent the rest of his life wandering around India and sharing his enlightened philosophy with the people. He died at the age of 80.

The Buddha organized his experiences into a doctrine known as the "Four Noble Truths." These truths state that all life is suffering, pain, and misery; that this suffering is caused by *tanha,* or selfish craving and personal desire; that happiness can be achieved by overcoming these cravings and desires; and that the way to overcome them is through the "eightfold path."

The eight steps are right knowledge, right intention, right speech, right behavior, right livelihood, right effort, right mindfulness, and right contemplation. When followed, according to the Buddha's teachings, these steps lead to the ultimate goal of *nirvana*—a state in which all desires are abolished and the self merges with infinity and the universe entire.

she completed and published a book on the subject, *Le Modernisme bouddhiste et le bouddhisme du Bouddha, (The Modern Buddhist and the Buddhism of Buddha.)* In her mind's ear, she could still hear echoes of the haunting Tibetan music that she had heard for the first time in northern India. Repeatedly, the theater of her mind projected visions of Mount Kanchenjunga in all of its snow-capped splendor.

Nearly two decades had passed since her visit to India. It had taken her that long to realize that what she wanted most in life was to return there. In India, she reasoned, she could advance her study of Far Eastern religions, particularly Buddhism, a religion that increasingly intrigued her. As a married woman, however, she no longer enjoyed the freedom of her youth. There was Néel to consider. She confessed to him that he did not measure up to the companion of her dreams. Nor was she the kind of wife he needed. He replied while David-Néel was in Lourdes. In an undated letter, he wrote:

> I don't know if you really understand me. I have a soul that is very bourgeois [middle class], and very stupid. A bourgeois life would have suited me. You are the antithesis [direct opposite] of that. Others have told you that, and they are right. Therefore, what shall we do with this relationship that we have created? . . . I am attached to you by legal ties easy to break, and by others out of habit. If your life with me is too difficult . . . I am willing to give you your liberty. . . . Tell me if you believe we should truly continue side by side, or if we should each go where the wind blows us.[39]

David-Néel felt torn between a comfortable married life and the lure of India and Tibet. At times, she felt a deep affection for Néel, but she also felt incapable of sharing her life with another person. She knew in her heart that she should never have entered into marriage, yet she could not bring herself to give up the security that marriage afforded her. She grappled with her dilemma until her dear Mouchy offered a solution. He proposed that she take "a long voyage" and offered to pay for it, hoping that finally she would flush her attraction for the Orient "out of her system."[40] She accepted.

In her last journal entry for 1910, David-Néel noted, "On the threshold of Nirvana—a good title for a book of travels across the Buddhist Orient."[41]

5

Affairs of the Heart and Soul

Et voilà, c'est fini . . . la vie continue. (It is finished. Life goes on.)
—Alexandra David-Néel, *Journal*

In mid-1911, David-Néel, now in her forty-third year, boarded the steamer *City of Naples* at Bizerte, Tunisia. The steamer slipped its moorings, eased into the stream, and headed for the open sea, and for points east of Suez and beyond. Néel watched her departure from the landing. He expected her to return in about a year. By then, he hoped, she would be ready to settle down and start acting like a more conventional kind of wife.

In her first letter to Néel, David-Néel wrote of observing his image "standing on the *quai* [quay or pier] of Bizerte, a silhouette I watched for such a long time, as it disappeared into the night." Then, as if trying to rationalize her compulsion to return to the Orient, she added, "My dearest Alouch, we are composed of many different cells, which pursue their lives in us, and how varied are the feelings that we experience."[42] She expected to return in 12 to 18 months, but Néel would not see her again for 14 years.

To characterize the marriage of Alexandra David-Néel and Philippe Néel as unusual would hazard an unparalleled understatement. Biographers, separated from this unique couple by time, space, and intimate knowledge, can only speculate as to the qualities that cemented their union. Might it be that both partners deeply honored their marriage vows? Whatever the truth, their marriage survived long years of separation and lasted until the death of one parted them. Although far away in body, Mouchy seemed ever present in spirit, and she wrote to him almost every day to pour out her joys, fears, and innermost feelings.

On her second trip to the Orient, David-Néel again began her journey at Ceylon, visiting Buddhist temples and studying the Pali language at the Theosophist center. After two months, she decided to move on again to India, this time via a comfortable steamer. She arrived in Tuticorin in the middle of the rainy season.

In 20 years, both India and David-Néel had changed. She had expected to find the India of her memory undisturbed and felt disappointed when she did not. The seasonal downpours added to her disappointment, blotting out the burning sun of her recollection and turning once dusty roads into rivers of mud. Still, this was what she had looked forward to for two decades, and she intended to make the most of her time in India. She immersed herself in her religious studies and continued to write.

She found modern Buddhists scarcer in India than in Paris. At Madurai, she spent some time with the dark-skinned Dravidians, who inhabit the south of India, and added to her knowledge of Hinduism and its rites and practices. Dravidians worship the Hindu trinity, or Trimurti, made up of Brahma, the creator; Vishnu, the preserver who takes on bodily form and substance from age to age to restore the balance of the world; and Shiva, the god of destruction and rebirth.

David-Néel felt more drawn toward Buddhism, which only then was beginning to make a comeback in the land of its origin, but she appreciated the contributions made by Hinduism to the religion of her choice. Some of their shared beliefs include the ideas of reincarnation, the process of birth and rebirth continuing for life after life, and *karma*, the effects of the actions of one life upon the next. "Having been born under conditions determined by his past deeds, it is for the man to overcome the difficulties caused by his mistakes, and to prepare better conditions for his present and his future lives," David-Néel wrote later. "In the same way it is important that he who is enjoying a happiness which he owes to his virtuous conduct in the past should beware of committing evil deeds that will involve him in suffering in the near, or distant, future."[43] Moving north along the Indian coast, David-Néel herself was about to experience a karmic incident.

While staying at the Theosophical Society headquarters in Adyar, David-Néel visited Pondicherry, all that remained of French India, to interview Sri Aurobindo Ghose, a former activist for Indian independence who had just converted to the role of spiritual leader. British authorities, still operating in a web of intrigue and deceit that originated during the "great game," continued to suspect him of antigovernment activities. The "great game" was a phrase coined by Rudyard Kipling to describe the contest for political supremacy in Central Asia among the British, Russians, and Chinese in the late nineteenth century. By virtue of "secret enquiries in Paris," [44] which had revealed information about David-Néel's radical background, the British suspected that she might be involved in a plot as an agent of the French or some other government.

Officials in Madras sent a warning to the governor of India, concluding with "It might be well therefore not to lose sight of her, and to inform the . . . criminal investigation department of Calcutta." [45] Throughout David-Néel's stay in Asia, British officials kept a wary eye on her activities, thwarting them whenever possible to the extent that outwitting the British became something of a challenge to her. The undue and unwanted attention paid to her by the British came as a direct result of her past actions as a young radical—karma in action.

During her stay at Adyar, David-Néel became fluent in several Asian languages, proficient in the art of photography, and even developed a considerable following of disciples who thought she was an *avatar* (goddess incarnate). In December, several devotees of Vishnu asked her to join them and become a true yogi, a practitioner of yoga (union) and the application of spiritual practices to achieve union of atman (self or soul) and Brahman (supreme self or soul). The Vishnuites approached her with their faces adorned with an ashen material that she readily recognized as "that sacred substance the cows emit naturally." [46] They invited her to live naked under a tree while devoting herself to attaining enlightenment. She gently declined their offer, explaining that her husband on another continent might not see the wisdom in such an arrangement.

By the end of the year, David-Néel had moved by train

HINDUISM

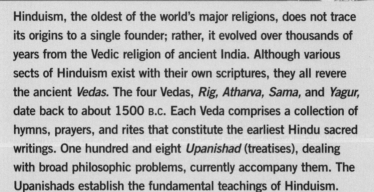

Hinduism, the oldest of the world's major religions, does not trace its origins to a single founder; rather, it evolved over thousands of years from the Vedic religion of ancient India. Although various sects of Hinduism exist with their own scriptures, they all revere the ancient *Vedas.* The four Vedas, *Rig, Atharva, Sama,* and *Yagur,* date back to about 1500 B.C. Each Veda comprises a collection of hymns, prayers, and rites that constitute the earliest Hindu sacred writings. One hundred and eight *Upanishad* (treatises), dealing with broad philosophic problems, currently accompany them. The Upanishads establish the fundamental teachings of Hinduism.

The Hindu religion embraces the concept that God exists and can be experienced in the depth of an individual's own being through achieving a transcendent state of consciousness, that is, a state that lies beyond ordinary limits. Hindus call this state *samadhi.* They believe that the purpose of life is to realize God, whether personified as Brahma or impersonalized in the neuter form of an absolute principal called Brahman.

A Hindu may worship one or more gods, goddesses, or none at all. The principal Hindu deities are Brahma, the creator; Vishnu, the preserver; and Shiva, the god of destruction and rebirth. Together, they form the *Trimurti,* the Hindu trinity. Innumerable lesser deities, including Shakti, the wife of Shiva, who is also called Devi exist and are worshipped by many Hindus. Shakti represents the female power of the universe and is believed to have existed since the beginning of time. The main branches of Hinduism are Vaishnavism, or worship of Vishnu, and Shaivism, worship of Shiva.

Most Hindus believe that the cycle of birth, death, and rebirth, known as *samsara,* defines a system of transmigration (reincarnation) whereby the effect of deeds (*karma*) in one life influences the next. Through the application of spiritual practices, Hindus hope to attain the union of Atman, or the individual self or soul, with Brahman, or the supreme self or soul, and thus release (*moksa* or *moksha*) from the cycle of rebirth (*samsara*).

to Calcutta. There, befriended by Sir John Woodruffe, justice of the high court and a devotee of Hinduism, she witnessed the inequities of the Hindu caste system. Within the system, the untouchables (members of the lowest category of Hindu society) lived in filth and abject poverty while the highest order of Brahmins luxuriated in opulence and enormous wealth. The caste system did not allow an untouchable to make physical contact with a member of a higher caste lest he or she contaminate a superior being.

David-Néel abhorred the system for its discriminatory practices and the Brahmins for suppressing Buddhism in the land of its origin, which resulted in reducing India to a virtual slave state at the time. Occasionally, when asked to speak, she lectured on Buddhist *dharma* (doctrine) as her way of countering the Brahmanic caste system that, in her view, lacked charity and compassion. Even so, she continued her studies in Sanskrit and Hinduism. Now and then, aided by the Woodruffes, she even participated in some of Hinduism's elaborate and exotic rituals. In her letters to Néel, David-Néel told her *"bien cher* [very dear] *Mouchy"*[47] that she was gathering research for a future book.

Toward the end of January 1912, David-Néel complained to Néel that she felt rushed, confused, and was suffering from dizzy spells. A month later, her mood had lifted to one of elation. She had received and accepted an offer to study at the esteemed Sanskrit college at Hardwar, on the Ganges. In the meantime, to escape the sweltering heat of Calcutta, she planned a visit to Sikkim on India's mountainous northern frontier. Néel, less than pleased at his wife's latest change of plans, demanded to know when she intended to come home. She replied that if he pressed her to return at once she would become a hermit and live in a cave in the Himalayas. He did not press her.

David-Néel's trip north by train took her across the verdant Bengal plain, past broad expanses of rice, bamboo thickets, and palm groves, emblazoned here and there by dabs of scarlet occasioned by the "flame of the forest" tree. At Siliguri, where she began to notice people of yellow skin with an Oriental cast to their eyes, she transferred to the narrow-gauge Darjeeling-Himalayan Railway and its famous Toy Train. The tiny engine chugged determinedly up the sharply ascending grade to the hill station of Darjeeling, whose elevation formed a lofty amphitheater.

Scanning the horizons, David-Néel could see the mountains of Sikkim rising in great tiers across the Rungeet River. In addition, far beyond them, she caught sight of the highlands of Tibet and marveled at the panoramic view of the magnificent, five-peaked Kanchenjunga, towering 28,000 feet above sea level. From this splendid and spectacular vantage point, she saw her future.

From Darjeeling, David-Néel decided to seek an audience with the thirteenth Dalai Lama, Thubten Gyatso, who was residing in Kalimpong, about 20 miles to the east. The Tibetan spiritual and civil leader was living under the protection of the British government in temporary exile from a brief Chinese occupation of Tibet (1910–1912). According to Sir Charles A. Bell, the British political officer in the Himalayas at the time, he matched the standard description of the Dalai Lama:

> He was regarded as a god, being an incarnation of Chen-re-zi, the Lord of Mercy, himself an emanation of Buddha. As Chen-re-zi is held to be the founder of the Tibetan race, and is worshipped as its patron deity, this gave the Dalai Lama an overpowering position in Tibet.[48]

To David-Néel's vast delight, she became the first woman to receive an audience with him.

"As I left Darjeeling, in the early rosy dawn of a cool spring morning, I little guessed the far-reaching consequences of my request," David-Néel wrote later, explaining, "I thought of a

The thirteenth Dalai Lama, the leader of the Tibetan people in both spiritual and civic matters, was living in exile when Alexandra David-Néel became the first woman to have an audience with him. The Dalai Lama was significantly impressed by David-Néel's astute understanding of Buddhism, considered rare for a Westerner. David-Néel left their meeting with the belief that the Dalai Lama had granted her permission to enter Lhasa.

short excursion, of an interesting but brief interview; while, actually, I became involved in wanderings that kept me in Asia for full 14 years."[49]

On April 15, 1912, the intense woman arrived at the home of the revered religious leader in a sedan chair, attired in a robe and wearing a veil. The worshipped one seemed amazed at the depth of David-Néel's knowledge about Buddhism. He believed that Westerners did not really understand the religion of Tibet. "It is precisely because I suspect that certain religious doctrines of Tibet have been misunderstood that I have come to you to be enlightened,"[50] she told him.

The Dalai Lama, a small man in a maroon robe and peaked yellow hat, obliged her, briefly answering David-Néel's questions orally and providing her with lengthy written answers later. The holy one invited her to correspond with him through Sir Charles if she had further questions. He ended their meeting saying, "Learn the Tibetan language."[51] She came away from her audience with the Dalai Lama convinced that he had cleared the way for her eventual entry into the Tibetan capital of Lhasa, also called the Forbidden City, where no Western woman had ever set foot.

While in Kalimpong, David-Néel stayed at a *dak* (traveler's rest house) originally located on post roads. By chance, a member of Sikkimese royalty, along with his attendants, was also staying there: Maharaj Kumar, the crown prince of Sikkim, Sidkeong Tulku. David-Néel's broadening fame as an Oriental religionist had reached the young prince. He invited her to meet with him, and she gladly accepted. She described Sidkeong to Néel in understated terms: "He is a young man, very agreeable, and appears to be extremely intelligent. He was magnificently dressed in gold brocade."[52]

David-Néel seemed careful not to appear overly enthusiastic in her description of Sidkeong, but the 43-year-old French-woman apparently felt a great attraction toward the 33-year-old

Sidkeong, both physically and intellectually. The Oxford-educated prince cut a handsome figure. Standing slightly taller than David-Néel, he looked at the world through deeply thoughtful almond eyes astride a strong nose, complemented by even features and a sensuous mouth. He wore his braided hair caught up in a silver clasp, and his presence exuded the confidence of someone used to command. His affinity for satins and embossed leather belts accentuated his princely air. Barbara Foster and Michael Foster went so far as to suggest that "Alexandra had met her prince charming." [53]

The prince immediately liked the French wanderer and invited her to his capital, Gangtok, about 28 miles northeast of Darjeeling. She said yes and he said, "Well, then, it is understood. I leave Dawasandup with you as interpreter. He will accompany you to Gangtok." [54] Sidkeong then went on ahead. Kazi Dawasandup, the prince's friend and confidante, was headmaster of the boarding school at Gangtok. David-Néel and Kazi made the trip to Gangtok on horseback in three days, shrouded in moving fogs. They arrived on April 22.

In Gangtok, David-Néel's relationship with Sidkeong blossomed into a deep and enduring friendship. Whether the pair, who were from opposite ends of the earth, ever entered into a romantic relationship remains open to question. Biographer Ruth Middleton noted, "It is unlikely that the nature of this friendship was other than platonic." Rather, Middleton went on, "He believed from the beginning that, closely associated in a previous life, they had chosen to continue their work together." [55] Regardless of the nature of their alliance, it unquestionably opened new paths to David-Néel in her pursuit of Buddhist knowledge.

At the prince's villa, David-Néel engaged in many long nighttime discussions about Buddhism with Sidkeong and his guests, which included yellow-hat and red-hat lamas. Yellow hats, who are celibate, represent the reformed branch of Mahayana Buddhism, which is the Buddhism headed by the

Dalai Lama and practiced in Tibet. Red hats form the older, less numerous branch, whose members may marry. Sidkeong was the titular head of the prevailing sect of Buddhism in Sikkim, known as the *Kagyü*.

During the short span of their relationship, the prince lavished David-Néel with precious gifts, gold and jeweled bracelets, earrings, rings, and other objects, and she became, according to Middleton, "his confidante, his traveling companion, his spiritual sister."[56] Throughout her long travels through unmapped Tibet, she would carry his jewelry on her person, refusing to part with a single item no matter how desperate her needs or situation became. When Sidkeong asked her to accompany him on an inspection tour of the outlying Buddhist monasteries, she consented, even though she knew it meant giving up her chance to become a Sanskrit scholar at Hardwar.

At the time, 67 monasteries existed in Sikkim. David-Néel and the prince first visited the Podang *gompa* (monastery) in early May 1912. David-Néel carried her camera and took photographs everywhere she went. Somewhere around this time, she met the *gomchen* (great hermit) of Lachen, the abbot of the monastery, at a court function in Gangtok. He would greatly influence her life in the near future. Over the next two years, David-Néel visited many more gompas with the prince, in the company of other orientalists, or on her own. She also visited Nepal as a guest of its maharaja.

On one of her excursions, she met the Dalai Lama for a second time, while he was returning to Tibet. The holy one visited with her briefly and invited her to continue their correspondence, via Sir Charles Bell, and to send him questions needing answers. As a memento of their second meeting, he gave her a white silk scarf. She wrote to Néel that she would cherish it as a *"souvenir de voyage."*[57] After her second meeting with the Dalai Lama, David-Néel commenced her study of Tibetan with a singular passion.

In March 1913, after a year of travel in Sikkim and

neighboring Nepal, David-Néel returned to the Ganges Valley and the holy city of Benares and resumed her scholarly study of Sanskrit and Vedanta (Hindu philosophy). There, she donned the saffron robe of a *sannyasin,* and received an honorary doctorate of philosophy from the College of Sanskrit. Toward year's end, a cholera epidemic erupted along the Ganges. At the same time, she received word that an apartment awaited her at the royal monastery of Sikkim. She packed her bags, folding cot, portable bathtub, and tent and left immediately for Gangtok.

For the new year of 1914, to honor David-Néel's scholarly accomplishments, the Sikkimese monks presented her with the robe of a lamina (female lama). They had duly consecrated the garment of dark red felt with a blue silk kimono-style collar and a yellow-fringed waistband. To complete her attire, they added a bonnet of golden Chinese silk and a pair of high Lhasa boots of leather and felt, embroidered with intricate patterns. The ensemble represented their acceptance of her in the rare society of devoted coreligionists.

In February, while David-Néel was tramping through the mountainsides, word of the death of Prince Sidkeong's father reached her and she returned at once to Gangtok. The prince's stepmother wanted her son, who was Sidkeong's half brother, to ascend to the throne, but Sidkeong, after a bitter familial struggle, took his rightful place as the Maharaja of Sikkim. Next, he had to decide whether to enter into a marriage of convenience with a Burmese princess, and he sought the advice of a seer. The oracle fell into a trance and, in an oddly soft voice, uttered an equally odd prophecy that Sidkeong need not concern himself about his marital dilemma. David-Néel resumed her travels in the high country.

In May 1914, Néel, who had repeatedly called for David-Néel's return, wrote that he had sold their villa in Tunis and had moved to the railway headquarters in Bône, Algeria. Furious that he had not consulted with her before selling the villa, regardless of the fact that *La Goulette* belonged to him or that she had given him no sign of returning home any time soon, she again threatened to become a hermit and move into a cave. Néel responded with another bank draft for her continuing financial stability.

Early that fall, David-Néel had planned to visit Bhutan. At the last moment, however, she had turned backed at the Bhutanese border and crossed instead into Tibet. She had finally succumbed to the lure of the majestic mountains at the "roof of the world," as Tibet is often called. Although forbidden passage into Tibet by the British, who still suspected her of clandestine activities, she made her way to Chörten Nyima, a remote Tibetan monastery set high among eagles' nests and sharp, clear air.

Legend holds that the secret writings of Padmasambhava are hidden at Chörten Nyima (sun shrine). Scholars consider Padmasambhava, the eighth-century founder of Buddhism in Tibet, to be the author of the *Bardo Thodol* and other important Tibetan Buddhist works. As the guest of four nuns at the dilapidated gompa, David-Néel added to her ever-increasing wealth of secret Buddhist knowledge and became increasingly fluent in Tibetan.

In the summer of 1914, David-Néel returned to the palace guesthouse in Gangtok, where she waited for funds to arrive from Néel. With the funds came word that war had broken out in Europe. The outbreak of World War I made it unsafe for her to return home. Instead, she spent much of the rest of the year wandering around the mountains with a friend and fellow orientalist and their company of servants.

In December, she informed Néel from Lachen, near the Tibetan frontier, that she had been accepted as a disciple of a renowned gomchen. Enthused, she wrote that her discipleship would advance her Buddhist studies immeasurably. Her enthusiasm turned to deep sorrow on December 6. David-Néel's journal entry for that day reads, "Sidkeong Tulku died

On her way to Bhutan, David-Néel made a sudden change of course and set up camp in Tibet, at the foot of the majestic Kangchenjunga Mountain, in 1914. Despite the fact that she was barred from entering Tibet by the British government, who suspected her of being a spy, David-Néel journeyed a great distance to an isolated Tibetan monastery high in the mountains.

at three o'clock in the afternoon."[58] The prince who had entered her life with unexpected suddenness had left it with brutish abruptness. Their affair, whether romantic or platonic, had ended.

In the cold winter of her soul, David-Néel turned to the gomchen of Lachen to help her through her deep despair.

6

Of *Gomchens* and Snow Leopards

One evening, the gomchen of Lachen appeared with all the trapping of a magician: a five-sided crown, a rosary-necklace made of one hundred and eight round pieces, cut out of so many skulls, an apron of human bones bored and carved, and in his belt the ritualistic dagger.

—Alexandra David-Néel, *Magic and Mystery in Tibet*

Sidkeong's death brought home to David-Néel the prophecy of the seer who had advised the maharaja that he need not concern himself with the marriage dilemma posed to him by the Burmese princess. The tragic resolution to Sidkeong's dilemma stunned and deeply aggrieved David-Néel, particularly because he had died of a mysterious, undiagnosed illness that much resembled poisoning. Suggestions of political intrigue and royal complicity surround his sudden death, but formal charges of foul play were never brought forward. How, and perhaps why, Sidkeong died will likely never be resolved.

At a tiny monastery in Lachen, in the high mountain passes just before Tibet, the gomchen of Lachen shared David-Néel's grief at Sidkeong's passing. He and the young maharaja had been fast friends. David-Néel had met him at a court function in Gangtok in 1912. His appearance—long, thick, braided hair that touched his heels; ears that dangled turquoise-studded earrings; and piercing eyes that glowed like hot embers—fascinated her. The local people held that the gomchen could work miracles, fly through the air, command demons, and kill men at a distance. "What an extraordinary man!"[59] she wrote.

Over the next two years, David-Néel visited the gomchen several times in Lachen and engaged him in conversations about Buddhism. Gradually, each developed a liking and respect for the other. Finally, in the early autumn of 1914, she approached him and asked to become his disciple. According to David-Néel, he protested, pointing out "that his knowledge was not extensive enough and that it was useless for me to stay in such an inhospitable region to listen to an ignorant man, when I had the opportunity of long talks with learned lamas elsewhere."[60] David-Néel persisted, and the gomchen finally assented.

The Frenchwoman and the hermit reached an agreement: She would teach him English and he would help improve her Tibetan. Later, if he deemed her worthy, he would reveal to her the secret oral teachings of tantric Buddhism. Buddhist tantrism is based on sophisticated ancient and medieval Sanskrit texts called *tantras*. It prescribes guidelines for meditation, rituals, and life orientation. Some *tantras* celebrate the body, esoteric geometric patterns, and sexuality as instrumental to transcendence.

The gomchen lived in a hideaway at De-chen called the Cave of Cear light. At 12,000 feet in the sky, the half-cave half-cabin hideaway overlooked the monastery at Lachen, which means "the big pass." David-Néel moved into a similar but smaller and less comfortable cave-cabin below the gomchen's quarters. It was here, in the high, clear air of the Himalayas, that a 14-year-old Tibetan boy named Aphur (Albert) Yongden became a leading figure in her life.

The stocky, bespectacled young man was one of her retinue of servants; he was also studying to become a lama in the red-hat sect of Mahayana (Tibetan) Buddhism. Over the next 40-plus years, Yongden would serve as David-Néel's faithful companion, researcher, collaborator, and fellow explorer. She would eventually adopt him as her son and name him as her heir.

In mid-November, the gomchen and David-Néel and her party moved down to the monastery at Lachen to spend the winter. The gomchen had business at the monastery and did not want to leave David-Néel alone and in inadequate quarters on the mountain. During the winter, David-Néel progressed amazingly with her Tibetan and began to speak with a proper Lhasan accent. She also made great progress in her studies of Buddhist metaphysics, a branch of philosophy dealing with the nature of existence and of truth and knowledge. The gomchen and his *chela* (disciple) sometimes exchanged information telepathically, that is, from one mind to the other without the use of speech, writing, gestures, and the like. David-Néel would later attempt to use telepathy occasionally to send messages "written on the wind."[61]

In the summer of 1915, the gomchen returned to his

Alexandra David-Néel met 14-year-old Aphur Yongden during her stay
with a gomchen who was teaching her tantric Buddhism in exchange
for English language instruction. The meeting of David-Néel and
Yongden, a student of the red-hat sect of Buddhist monks, marked
the beginning of relationship that would last more than 40 years.

mountain retreat to prepare for the next winter. David-Néel
joined him. Local laborers improved her cave by adding a second-
story wooden structure to it. The view from her cave-cabin

looked straight out at the five peaks of Kanchenjunga, which, wrote Barbara Foster and Michael Foster, is "called the store-house of the treasures of the gods because its snows were first to reflect dawn's gold and last to don the sable of night."[62] In this isolated setting, occasionally in the company of a stray bear or snow leopard, the French Buddhist resumed her search for meaning, delving into the psychic discoveries that she would later describe in her book *Magic and Mystery in Tibet.*

David-Néel's progress in her quest for knowledge came gradually and at a price. She suffered now and again from the pain of rheumatism, fever, nausea, and a recurrence of her neurasthenia. By Christmas Eve 1915, she felt wrapped in despair and enormously homesick, but as she always seemed to do, she shook off her ailments, both physical and mental, and plodded down the path toward enlightenment a step at a time.

As David-Néel's strength increased, she experimented with *tumo* breathing and *lung-gom* walking. *Tumo* breathing employs techniques of autosuggestion and breath retention to focus on the fire within, enabling *tumo* practitioners to survive extreme cold. *Lung-gom* walking involves a walker fixating on a distant goal and entering a trancelike state until the walker experiences a sensation comparable to flying. These Tibetan practices would serve her in good stead in the future.

In the summer of 1916, David-Néel's isolation and disciple-ship with the gomchen of Lachen ended. Her mentor bestowed on her the Tibetan name "Lamp of Wisdom." In the course of her studies, the gomchen had often recounted his travels in Tibet as a younger man and had thereby familiarized his French disciple with the land's geography, people, and customs. He advised her to continue her education on the road as a pilgrim and to impart what she had learned to the entire world.

Many years later, she would document much of what she had learned from the gomchen in her book *The Secret Oral Teachings in Tibetan Buddhist Sects,* written with Lama Yongden. English-born Buddhist scholar Alan Watts called it "the most direct, no-nonsense, and down-to-earth explanation of Mahayana Buddhism which has thus far been written."[63] *Oral Teachings* leaves the reader with many points to reflect on, not least of which are these:

> To *believe* that one *knows* is the greatest of the barriers which prevent *knowledge*. . . . The attitude which these teachings advocate is one of a strong will to know all that is possible to know, never halt on the road to investigation which extends infinitely far before the feet of the explorer.[64]

Long before David-Néel wrote these words, her own investigations were only beginning. In the years to come, her works would be translated into all major languages and read by millions. In July 1916, as she and Yongden set out for the busy market town of Shigatse in south-central Tibet as part of her pilgrimage, David-Néel's education was a work in progress.

The Panchen Lama, who was the abbot of Tashilhunpo monastery and rival of the Dalai Lama, had heard of David-Néel, the French Buddhist, and had invited her to visit with him. According to Sir Charles Bell, British resident officer in Sikkim, because of a complex succession of incarnations, "it is held by many Tibetans that the Panchen Lama is spiritually higher than the Dalai."[65] In journeying to Shigatse, David-Néel knew that she was risking the wrath of the British resident, but she felt that a meeting with the Panchen Lama was worth almost any risk.

During her short visit, David-Néel impressed the Panchen Lama greatly. He fully affirmed her Tibetan name, "Lamp of Wisdom," and she endeared herself to his mother. She engaged in many stimulating dialogues with the 3,800 monks in Tashilhunpo. The Panchen Lama invited her to stay at the monastery, but she did not want to be caught in the middle of the rivalry between the two high lamas and politely declined. When she left in August 1916, the Panchen Lama presented her with the robe of a graduate lama and an honorary doctorate from the Tashilhunpo university. The lama's mother would continue to write to her for many months afterward.

When David-Néel and Yongden returned to De-chen, they found the hermitage in shambles and the gomchen in retreat, refusing to see anyone. Charles Bell had learned of David-Néel's trip into Tibet and had fined the people of Lachen, the closest village, even though the villagers had nothing to do with her travels. Looters from the village, hoping to find valuables among her belongings, had ransacked her dwelling. Sir Charles subsequently fined David-Néel and ordered her to leave Sikkim within 14 days.

Angered at her treatment by the British, David-Néel promised revenge. "These uncivilized proceedings made me wish to retaliate," she wrote later, "but in a witty way, befitting the spirit of the great city in which I had the privilege of being born." [66] With her expulsion from Sikkim, she vowed to return to Tibet and became more determined than ever to become the first white woman to enter its capital, Lhasa.

At the monastery at Lachen, Yongden gathered all of David-Néel's belongings and packed them in her 28 cases. He now became the dominant, and some might say the most dominated, male in her life. The son of a petty official, he had served a Sikkimese nobleman in exchange for a little education. He wanted to become a man of the world. David-Néel had grown fond of Yongden and offered him travel, adventure, and six rupees a month to extend his employment. He accepted, and the unlikely pair commenced a 40-year relationship that was heavy on travel and adventure but sometimes light on rupees.

On September 2, 1916, David-Néel, sad at heart for having to leave her beloved mountain sanctuary, and Yongden left Lachen for the last time. They proceeded to the bustling Bengalese port of Calcutta, where they stayed for several weeks.

Alexandra David-Néel in Her Own Words and Photographs

From Alexandra David-Néel's
My Journey to Lhasa

Until then our journey through the Po country had been perfectly peaceful, and I began to think that there must be much exaggeration in the stories which are current about the Popas [inhabitants of Po].

Popas—so Thibetans say—are born robbers. Each year gangs, sometimes to the number of a hundred, fall unexpectedly on their neighbours of the Kong-bu or Dainshi provinces and loot their villages. Beside these organized expeditions, most Popas—traders, pilgrims, or mere villagers—find it difficult to let any traveler they may happen to meet on their way pass without trying to levy an undue tax on his baggage, however miserable it may be. A few handfuls of barley flour, a worn-out blanket, two or three copper coins—all is good to

them. But if, as a rule, they let the poor folk who meekly submit to their demands go unmolested, they are quick to turn murderers when resistance is offered or a valuable booty is expected.

Truly, no wealthy travellers venture to go through the forests of Po. Only the poorest of the poor—the beggar pilgrims made bold by the fact of their utter destitution—are to be met along the tracks which cross the Popas' hill.

As for us, we had not met any outsider, either rich or poor, on our way. The few people whom we had seen on the solitary roads were all natives of the country, or settlers who had practically become Popas.

Events were now to take another turn, and that gay New Year marked the end of a period of quietness.

[One afternoon] we passed by an isolated farm just as a number of people were emerging from it. The New Year festivities were still going on; some of the men who had enjoyed themselves were decidedly drunk, and the remainder were not very sober. All of them carried guns across their shoulders, and some made a pretense of shooting at us. As for us, we proceeded as if we had noticed nothing.

In the evening I discovered a

roomy cave in which we slept comfortably. We slept much too long, and delayed still further over some soup at breakfast. As we did so, a man appeared and asked us if we had nothing to sell. He regarded the contents of our bags, which were still open.

Our two common spoons especially attracted his attention. Then he seated himself, and taking a piece of dried, fermented cheese out of his dress he began to eat it.

That kind of cheese is very much like French Roquefort. Thinking it would improve our menus, Yongden asked the man if he had some to sell. He answered in the affirmative; he had some at home, not far from the cave, and would barter one against needles, if we had any. We had a few which we had carried for this purpose. So the man went to fetch his cheese.

We had not yet finished our packing when he came back with a cheese and followed by another man. The newcomer was much bolder than the first with whom we had dealt. He fingered the cloth of our tent and told us that he would purchase it. He then took the spoons and examined them, while his companion cast glances in the direction from which they had come, as if expecting other arrivals.

We had no doubt about the intentions of the two Popas. The bolder one had already put the two coveted spoons in his *amphag* [breast pocket] and refused to give them back, while the other one endeavored to take the tent out of the lama's hands.

I realized that others had been summoned and were to assist in the robbery.

The matter would soon become serious. We must frighten these two away and start in haste. Perhaps we would be able to reach the next village, and the thieves would not dare to follow us.

I endeavoured to appeal to the good feelings of the men, but it was of no avail. Time was of importance; we must put an end to the business, and show the others that we were not timid and defenceless folk.

"Let that tent alone at once!" I commanded. "And give the spoons back!"

In the meantime I had my revolver in readiness under my dress. The boldest of the thieves only laughed and, turning his back on me, he bent to pick up some other object. I shot, from close behind him, turning my revolver away from him. But his companion saw me and, being too terrified to warn his friend, he could do nothing but stare wildly at me. Whether or not the other fellow saw him, I cannot tell, but he threw himself backwards just as I shot, and the bullet passed close to his head, grazing his hair.

C

Flinging the spoons and the tent on the ground, the two ran like hunted hares across the thicket.

The situation was not entirely pleasant. The ruffians might have gone to fetch some of their kindred, the men whom they seemed to expect. I told Yongden to tie the loads in haste and be off as quickly as possible.

What would have happened, had we remained alone, I cannot say, for a party of about thirty pilgrims—the first foreign travellers we met in Po *yul* [country], and the only ones we were ever to meet—suddenly appeared. They had heard the shot, and enquired as to its cause.

It was annoying to be identified as carrying a revolver, for only chiefs and traders own these. Of course they thought that it was Yongden who had fired; and later on when they asked to see the weapon, we produced and old-pattern small one, instead of the automatic pistol that had nearly sent the Popa on to another world.

We joined the party, and perhaps we owe our lives to this most unexpected meeting.

Alexandra David-Néel crosses the border into Tibet for the first time in 1912. During this period, David-Néel would become the companion and confidante of Sidkeong Tulku, the crown prince of Sikkim, a kingdom on the border of Tibet. David-Néel's relationship with the young prince would contribute immensely to her developing knowledge of Buddhism.

D

At the border of Tibet in 1914, Alexandra David-Néel pauses to build a *chorten*, or shrine, made of stones.

E

Alexandra David-Néel, third from the left, and Sidkeong Tulku, fifth from the left, traveled together throughout Sikkim in 1912. The pair toured many monasteries and met with numerous yogis during their time together. Sidkeong would later become the maharaja, or king, of Sikkim.

The monks in this photo of Phodang monastery in Sikkim, one of the many that David-Néel visited with Sidkeong Tulku, perform a Buddhist ritual or *puja*. David-Néel's interaction with the many Buddhist monks she met in Sikkim greatly influenced her already impressive understanding of the religion.

The 14-year-old Aphur Yongden was studying to become a red-hat Buddhist lama when Alexandra David-Néel met him in Lachen in 1914. The two became increasingly close companions over the next 40 years; David-Néel would eventually adopt the young boy as her son.

Alexandra David-Néel was 69 years old when she took this picture in Hankow Harbor, China, as she journeyed away from air raids conducted by the Japanese. David-Néel spent eight years (1937–1945) in China during the Sino-Japanese War.

H

Néel continued to press for her return, but she continued to put him off, promising to return home via Japan, which she lauded as "modern, intelligent, and peaceful."[67] The travelers left Calcutta on November 6, 1916. After brief stops in Burma and Indochina, where they toured Buddhist monasteries and holy places, they arrived in Kobe, Japan, on February 7, 1917. The following month, in a letter to Néel, David-Néel wrote:

> I was disappointed in Japan, but everything would have disappointed me in my state of mind. I cannot deny Atami offers charming sites; upon my return by rail, I went through lovely mountainous regions, but there are very similar landscapes in the Cervennes, the Pyrenees, or the Alps (in France)[,] whereas the Himalayas are unique.[68]

Before her visit to Japan, David-Néel had just come down from three years on the roof of the world, where the living was simple and harsh and she had loved every minute of it; the cold of the country did not compare with the cold that now chilled her heart. Continuing her letter to her dear Mouchy, she confessed:

> Truthfully, I am "homesick" for a land that is not mine. I am haunted by the steppes, the solitude, the everlasting snow and the great blue sky "up there[.]" The difficult hours, the hunger, the cold, the wind slashing my face, leaving me with enormous, bloody, swollen lips. The camp sites in the snow, sleeping in the frozen mud, none of that counted, those miseries were soon gone and we remained perpetually submerged in a silence, with only the song of the wind in the solitude, almost bare even of plant life, the fabulous chaos of rock, vertiginous peaks and horizons of blinding light. A land that seems to belong to another world, a land of Titans or gods? I remained under its spell.[69]

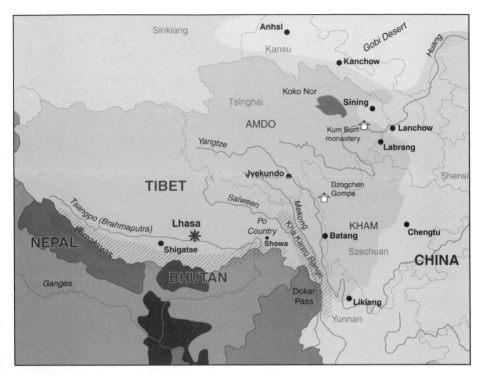

The location of Tibet, just west of China and north of India and Nepal, enabled David-Néel and her companion Aphur Yongden to travel to countries throughout the East, including India, China, Japan, and Korea.

Japan lacked the ethereal qualities of the land of snows that had so captivated the heart of the French Buddhist. When a bank draft from Néel, who had accepted a better paying position as director of the l'Ouenza mines in North Africa, arrived in July, David-Néel and her Tibetan companion left Kobe immediately for the mountainous land of Korea, perhaps hoping to find another Tibet.

In Korea, the travelers stayed at several monasteries. They found some cool, clear air in the mountains there, but mostly they found lots and lots of rain. On fair days, David-Néel tramped the mountain paths; when it rained, she meditated indoors. Tibet never left her thoughts for more than a few minutes. She began to plan her return to the land of her childhood dreams. A return through India was out of the question, of course, but the vast Chinese frontier bordering on Tibet seemed to invite infiltration. That was it, she decided. She would return to Tibet through China.

David-Néel and Yongden paused in Seoul long enough to renew their passports, then, financed by another bank draft from Néel, boarded a train bound for Peking, China. To David-Néel's way of thinking, there was more than one way to skin a snow leopard.

7

Wind Song

When a girl, I could remain for hours near a railway line, fascinated by the glittering rails and fancying the many lands toward which they led. But . . . my imagination did not evoke towns, buildings, gay crowds, or stately pageants; I dreamed of wild hills, immense deserted steppes and impassable landscapes of glaciers.
—Alexandra David-Néel, *My Journey to Lhasa*

David-Néel and Yongden arrived in Peking in October 1917.
David-Néel's plan called for them to travel 1,800 miles across western China to Kum Bum, the "Monastery of 100,000 Images." The monastery is located southeast of Koko Nor, the famous blue lake in disputed territory along the Chinese-Tibetan border. Her entry into Tibet and her subsequent travels in the land of snows was to be made without the knowledge of and against the will of both the Dalai Lama in Lhasa and Sir Charles Bell at Gangtok. By chance, in Peking, David-Néel met a rich Tibetan lama from Kum Bum. She gladly accepted his offer to join his caravan for his long return trip home.

In the winter of 1917, David-Néel received another bank draft from Néel and news of her mother's death a year earlier. As recipient of her mother's estate, David-Néel immediately sent her will to Néel, leaving the bulk of her net worth to him and instructing him to provide for Yongden. The two wanderers joined the lama and headed west on the caravan trail in January 1918. Their journey through a land rife with banditry and civil war and riddled with disease proved both difficult and dangerous. Civil strife in China had commenced with the collapse of the Manchu dynasty in 1911–1912 and continued off and on until the final Communist victory in 1949. In *Magic and Mystery in Tibet*, David-Néel recounted some of her experiences while en route to Kum Bum:

> I become acquainted with civil war and robbery. I endeavour to nurse wounded men left without help. One morning I see a bunch of heads—those of newly beheaded robbers—hung above the door or our inn. That sight arouses philosophical thoughts about death in my placid son [Yongden], which he quietly expounds to me.[70]

On another occasion, the travelers found themselves in a village under siege, where she "could watch storming enemies climbing the city walls on high ladders, while defenders hurled stones down on them."[71] A more insidious enemy struck David-Néel in yet another village when she contracted the plague of the dreaded pulmonary variety that had ravaged Europe in the fourteenth century. Miraculously, after battling the disease for four days, her fever broke and she recovered.

On July 12, 1918, after six months on the road contending with untold hardships and life-threatening situations, David-Néel and Yongden arrived at their destination. In her first letter to dear Mouchy, she wrote, "Auff I've reached Kumbum [sic]!"[72] At Kum Bum, the weary travelers settled into comfortable quarters in a charming Chinese-style building surrounding a patio, where they set to work translating Buddhist manuscripts. David-Néel viewed her task as one of helping unlock the door to Eastern thought to the Western mind.

The great monastery at Kum Bum stands on the place where Tsong Khapa, the founder of the yellow-hat reforms, was born in 1555, in the Amdo region of eastern Tibet, now part of China. Legend has it that a miraculous tree grew from the spot where his mother delivered him. The tree later bore leaves with images of various deities and the six syllables *Aum Mani Padme Hum* (hundred thousand images).[73] Thus the origin of the name Kum Bum by which the monastery became known. David-Néel and Yongden based themselves at Kum Bum, the inspiration for James Hilton's Shangri-La in his classic *Lost Horizon,* for the next two and a half years.

Travelers routinely visited the monastery to pay homage to Tsong Khapa. These visits often occasioned special feasts. David-Néel especially enjoyed "a certain Mongolian dish made of mutton, rice, Chinese dates, butter, cheese curds, sugar candy, and various other ingredients and spices, all boiled together."[74] Such dishes offered a welcome relief from the usual fare of *tsampa* (barley gruel) and Tibetan-style tea brewed with butter and salt. Central Asian peasants believed that the regular consumption of barley gruel would guarantee a favorable status in future rebirths. David-Néel also eagerly partook of savory *momos* (meat wrapped in a ball of baked paté and steamed.) Such cuisine spared the partaker from the Tibetan caveat "To eat lama's food requires jaws of iron."[75]

In the fall of 1918, both David-Néel, now 50 years old, and Yongden contracted the influenza that was ravaging the world during 1918–1919. While laid low with high fevers, word of the war's end reached them in November. After regaining their health and strength, they sewed together panels of red, white, and blue cloth to create a makeshift French tricolor with an embroidered inscription. They carried the banner to the top of a nearby mountain, unfurled it, and waved it gloriously for all below to see. The banner's inscription proclaimed a common Tibetan prayer of thanks: *"Lha gyalo! De tamche pam!"* ("Victory to the Gods! The demons are vanquished!").[76]

In the spring of 1919, despite the accelerating civil war, David-Néel led a short expedition to explore the Koko Nor region northwest of Kum Bum as a warm-up for a much longer excursion that she was planning. "I departed in secret, as dawn broke," she wrote later,

> leading my small caravan across the immense Tibetan solitudes; barren deserts and grassland deserts, equally silent, wild, mysterious, harsh, dramatic uplands, realm of dreams, terra incognita [unknown or unexplored land].[77]

As in most of the forbidden land of Tibet, dangers lurked all about. Foreigners had been known to disappear without a trace in the vast regions. David-Néel stayed constantly vigilant and kept her little revolver handy in her saddlebag, ready at all times to voice the common greeting to strangers: "No closer, friend, or I'll shoot!"[78] This particular venture went well, however, and David-Néel's party returned to Kum Bum with gifts of ceremonial scarves and butter from a local sorcerer.

Back at Kum Bum, a virtual treasure trove of sacred manuscripts, David-Néel turned her attention from translating rare writings to a deep form of meditation. She shut herself off in *tsams* (boxlike structures once maintained on the outskirts of monasteries) and began experimenting with some of the mysteries of Tibet. During one excursion into the world of esoteric happenings, she created a *tulpa* (a phantom being voluntarily produced by powerful concentration of thought and the repetition of prescribed rites). She later vaguely defined the process as actualized by an enlightened being this way:

> The mind unflinchingly fixed on his aim, indifferent to the various mirages and allurements of the roadside, this man controls the forces begotten by his concentration of mind and his bodily activity. Death may dissolve his body on the path, but the psychic energy of which that body is both creator and instrument, will remain coherent. Pushing forward towards the same goal, it will provide itself with a new material instrument, that is to say, with a new form, which is a *tulku*.[79]

David-Néel acknowledged that opinions differ as to just how this phenomenon occurs: Some lamas believe that this energy attracts compatible elements to form a new being; others suggest that the disembodied force enters an existing being whose mental and material disposition acquired in past lives blends with the released coherent energy to form a compatible union. In any case, the Dalai Lama represents the ultimate tulku.

In the fall of 1920, crops failed in western China, a cholera epidemic raged in Chengtu in nearby Szechuan province, and local governors-turned-warlords began fighting and pillaging among one another. David-Néel and Yongden continued their studies through the early winter of 1920–1921, with Yongden concentrating on becoming a monk by means of a special examination. Meanwhile, his companion busied herself translating part of *The Diamond Sutra,* a 100-volume work by Nagarjuna, the sixth-century Buddhist scholar whose writings formed a bridge between Sanskrit and the northern languages. At the same time, the political situation started deteriorating in Central Asia as the Russian civil war spread to Mongolia and the fighting heated up along the Chinese-Tibetan border.

In February 1921, David-Néel, having been prohibited from joining the holy order at Kum Bum because she was a woman, decided that the time had come at last to move on. Néel demanded that she come home, for they had now been separated for nearly a decade. David-Néel again turned her back on his demands. A greater demand beckoned her. She still felt "haunted by the song of the wind in the solitude," [80] and the wind kept whispering "Lhasa."

8

The Gods
and Alexandra

As we advanced, the Potala grew larger and larger. Now we
could discern the elegant outlines of its many golden roofs.
They glittered in the blue sky, sparks seeming to spring from
their sharp upturned corners, as if the whole castle, the glory
of [Tibet], had been crowned with flames.
—Alexandra David-Néel, *My Journey to Lhasa*

On February 5, 1921, David-Néel again led a small party out of Kum Bum at dawn: destination Lhasa. This time, David-Néel and Yongden, who was now a lama, would roam the unforgiving wildernesses of Central Asia for almost three years. Although their wanderings appeared haphazard, the circuitous route that they followed was influenced by many factors beyond her control, including artificial restrictions imposed by the British, Chinese, and Tibetan governments; money; bandits; pestilence; civil disorders; and a host of lesser deterrents to a more direct path. Despite the hardships and perils accompanying their travels, however, David-Néel never forgot for a moment that her true goal was Lhasa.

David-Néel led her small party, Yongden, four loyal servants, a horse, and seven mules, eastward to Sining, herself astride a "great black mule." [81] In Sining, a Christian missionary cashed a bank draft for her and the party headed south through Kansu and Szechuan provinces, traveling in Chinese territory so as not to conflict with British or Tibetan officials. David-Néel led the way, serving as a scout for her tiny party and interacting with Goloks and Khampas. She described the inhabitants of the Tibetan regions of Golok and Kham as "gentlemen brigands," [82] which is another way of saying "polite robbers." Many Central Asians lived at least in part off their plunders. To add to their concerns, travelers in these areas could routinely expect to encounter famine, cholera, tigers, and leopards.

David-Néel, a master of disguises, traveled as a *dakini* (mother goddess). Dressed as a Tibetan nun, replete with a sacred necklace of 108 pieces of human skull, she felt right at home on the Asian steppes. She thought like a Buddhist because she *was* one, and her holy aspect helped to see her through more than a few threatening situations on the road. Yongden added to her mystique, playing tunes on a tiny whistle to spread the word in villages that his "mother" was an ancient sorcerer. At age 52, David-Néel fought off the pain of arthritis and the gloom of depression day in and day out, but her iron will and the power of her dream drove her on.

David-Néel's party arrived at Dzogchen gompa in Kham, near the Yangtze River, in September 1921. After dining with the rich abbot of the monastery on a Chinese-style reverse menu consisting of dessert first, followed by dumplings, stews, fish, meat, and concluding with soup, David-Néel took sick with enteritis, an inflammation of the intestines. She decided to continue farther south on the Yangtze to seek medical attention at the mission in Bhatang, but when a minor Chinese official denied her passage for lacking the proper travel authorization, she diverted her party's course to Jyekundo.

Jyekundo stands at the edge of the Chang Tang (desert of grass), set amid white-topped mountains in the central Amdo region of Tibet. David-Néel and her companions arrived there in October. Although they made two attempts to leave, one toward the north and one to the south, heavy snow and Tibetan authorities, respectively, thwarted their efforts.

In June 1922, the British General Sir George Pereira, passed through the garrison-like town on his way to Lhasa while on a secret mission for his government. David-Néel befriended him, and he rewarded her friendship by sharing his valuable maps with her. Sir George, tracing what he thought to be the course of the Po River on his map, confided, "My information is that there are several accessible passes above the springs, where the river rises. If you went that way to Lhasa, you would be the first." [83] He went on his way in July, and she left with her party to return to Sining the next month, arriving in Kanchow, northwest of Sining, in November.

In January 1923, David-Néel continued to direct her group to the northwest, and they reached Anhsi in the Gobi Desert in March, before turning back for Kanchow and Lanchow. So far, David-Néel had led her party far afield of her intended destination. Some observers believe that she realized that this journey represented her last grand adventure and that she wanted to make it last as long as possible. She possibly also felt uneasy about a reunion with her spouse after so long a separation. Whatever her motivations for pressing on to Lhasa, however circuitously, they surely included sweet revenge against the British, fame, acclaim, and the makings of an incredible story, which would see print as *My Journey to Lhasa*.

Heading south again in May 1923, David-Néel led her band across the dry, dusty land of Kansu. Continuing, they passed through Chengtu, Szechuan, and traversed muddy roads, raging rivers, and combat zones caused by a resurgence of the Sino-Tibetan war to arrive in Likiang, Yunnan, in late September. Finally, swinging northwest, they arrived at Abbé Ouvrard's Christian parish on the right bank of the Mekong River in October 1923. In defiance of the British government and the Dalai Lama, Alexandra David-Néel at last stood poised for a serious run at reaching Lhasa, 500 to 600 miles to the west.

On October 24, 1923, David-Néel dismissed her servants, and she and Lama Yongden, now a man of 24 years, left the mission on the Mekong on the last leg of their journey. "Farewell . . . we have turned the corner of the road," David-Néel recounted later, "and the Mission House is out of sight. The adventure begins." [84]

By then, David-Néel had perfected her Tibetan and had devised a simple plan to aid them on their way to the Forbidden City. She and Yongden disguised themselves as beggarly pilgrims. David-Néel dyed her hair black with Chinese ink and added braids of yak hair to it. Beneath her robe, she hid her valuables, a compass, and a revolver. To complete her deception, she darkened her skin with cocoa, blackened her hands with soot, and adopted the role of a medium.

With them, they brought little more than a small tent and a teakettle. Shunning blankets and extra clothes, each carried a begging cup and a pair of chopsticks. On good days, they subsisted on a poor Tibetan peasant's fare of boiled barley and tea with a little butter and salt in it; on bad days, they made do with nothing. To avoid discovery, she and Yongden would sleep by day and travel only at night, skirting the main caravan route and following an obscure and treacherous route.

"Many travelers had been stopped on the way to Lhasa, and had accepted failure. I would not," she noted later. "I would reach Lhasa and show what the will of a woman could achieve!"[85] With this kind of determination, she set out for Dokar Pass in the Kha Karpo Range, the snow mountains that guard the southeastern entrance to Tibet.

The two travelers, dressed in Chinese garb, approached Dokar Pass through a pleasant valley coated white with frost. It grew colder as they trekked higher. At the pass, a blizzard welcomed them to the land of snows, as if to foretell of events to come. "*Into what mad adventure am I about to throw myself*,"[86] David-Néel wondered at the threshold of Tibet. Before descending the steep decline, the pilgrims paused to honor the timeless tradition of Tibetan travelers. Facing in turn the four cardinal points—north, south, east, and west—they shouted in unison, "May all beings find happiness."[87] Moving on, they descended and trudged across a vast blanket of whiteness that seemed to stretch endlessly before them.

After crossing the silvery expanse, they paused to look back. "Behind extended the waste I had crossed," David-Néel wrote years later, adding,

> In front of me was a precipitous fall of the mountain.
> The moon rose [and] the impassive landscape . . .
> seemed to awaken under the blue light . . . sparks

glittered to and fro, and faint sounds were wafted by
the wind.[88]

At dawn, exhausted, they pitched their little tent in a sheltered
place and slept.

Along the way, Yongden used his status as a red-hat lama
to cadge food from other pilgrims and called on his knowledge
of the occult arts to solicit lodging and other favors from
villagers. He often performed *mo* (telling fortunes by counting
beads or staring into a bowl of water) to great advantage
among superstitious Tibetans. As an added assurance of their
safe passage, Yongden proclaimed to wayfarers that David-Néel
was a *sang yum* (spouse of a tantric wizard). Few travelers
wanted to risk the ire of a wizard of any kind.

Ten days out from Abbé Ouvrard's mission, they reached
the Salween River and entered into lower Tsangpo Valley,
where Burma meets Assam on the frontier of India. Captain
Eric Bailey, who had surveyed and mapped this region for
the government of India in 1913, had complained of leeches
that flourished there and of "every species of fly which bit or
stung."[89] David-Néel and Yongden found the lower-life
inhabitants of the region no less abundant.

They pressed on west. Soon they traversed Tondo-la
(pass) at 11,200 feet and tramped on through great forests
and shallow valleys, sharing the lands with a variety of
wildlife. One night, David-Néel awakened to find herself
almost nose to nose with a leopard. She remained calm. Years
before, in India, she had experienced a similar encounter
with a Bengal tiger and had remained motionless until the
tiger left. Speaking softly so as not to awaken Yongden, she
murmured, "Little friend, I have been closer to a greater
prince of the jungle than you. Be on your way quietly."[90] The
leopard left.

One day, a sentry accosted the two pilgrims. Posted by
Lhasa to question suspicious travelers, the guard demanded

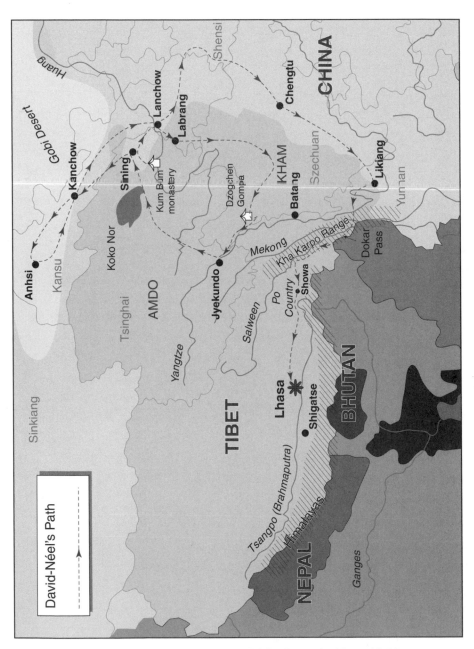

After a long and difficult journey, David-Néel finally reached her goal, Lhasa,
becoming the first Western woman to enter Tibet's "Forbidden City."

to know where they were bound and where they had been. Yongden, who had already told the story that he and his mother were returning home to the Amdo region from a pilgrimage to the snow mountains, repeated the tale. The gombo believed him and handed him a rupee as alms. In moderate haste, they moved on to To-la, the next pass on their tortuous route.

Ascending to the heights of To-la, they found an array of prayer flags, marking the summit of a pass. They paused only long enough to look skyward and shout the traditional salutation: *"Lha gyalo! De tamche pam!"*[91] Descending into the Salween Valley, they lingered only briefly before striking out for uncharted territory.

One day soon thereafter, David-Néel and her "son" reached the high gorge through which the Giamo Nu River flows. Looking down at the winding ribbon of water several thousand feet below did not alarm David-Néel, but she felt a twinge of concern about the means for crossing the gorge, "a single cable fastened to poles fixed at both ends at the same level, and it sagged terrifyingly."[92] Later, David-Néel described her chasm crossing this way:

> [A Tibetan] girl and I were bound with rough straps, and tied together to a wooden hook that would glide on the leather cable. . . . [A] push sent us swinging in the void, like two pitiable puppets.
>
> In less than one minute, we were down in the middle of the dip, and then, from the other bank, the ferrymen began their work. Each jerk they gave at the towing rope caused us to dance in the air a most unpleasant kind of jig.[93]

Then the towing rope broke. David-Néel took the ominous setback with Buddhalike passivity, but the young Tibetan girl turned pale and her eyes grew wide with fright.

She looked at the point where the strap that bound them together was affixed to the hook. Trembling, she said, "The strap is coming loose."[94]

In what seemed like an interminably long time to the dangling pair, a ferryman worked his way toward them along the sagging cable, "hands and feet up, the way flies walk on the ceiling,"[95] with another towrope. David-Néel told him about the loose strap but he saw nothing wrong with it. "I hope it will hold fast until you arrive at the bank,"[96] he said. David-Néel fumed.

"He hoped. . . . Bless the fellow! I also 'hoped,'"[97] she exclaimed. With that much hope working for them, the two "pitiable puppets" finally made it safely to the far side. Yongden protested his mother's harrowing experience to the ferrymen, and they appeased the two pilgrims with a bountiful share of their food. The pilgrims continued west toward Po yul.

In late December, David-Néel and Yongden traversed Aigni-la. On the far side of the pass at its base, David-Néel discovered one of the feeder springs of the Tsangpo River. Delighted with her find, she decided to search for additional springs. When it began to snow, Yongden did not share her delight. After being caught in a severe winter storm, they stumbled onto a cave where they took temporary shelter. When they attempted to continue their journey the next day, Yongden fell into a ravine and injured his leg. They returned to the cave.

When Yongden could not walk the following day, David-Néel set out for help. After searching the area, she found no help and started back for the cave. In the vast, undisturbed whiteness and gathering darkness, she became disoriented and fell exhausted in the snow. As the night closed in around her, the situation looked grim for David-Néel.

"I was on the point of shouting to the lama when I discerned a small light a little higher up," David-Néel recalled later. "No doubt Yongden was there and he had lighted, to guide me, the roll of taper [waxed wick] which we had in our bag."[98] That indeed turned out to be the case, and the pair averted another potential disaster.

Yongden's leg injury improved enough for him to walk with the aid of a crude crutch the next day, and the pilgrims resumed their westward trek. The heavy snows that had fallen for 65 straight hours finally ceased. They accepted it as a favorable omen, but on Christmas Eve 1923, Yongden succumbed to a high fever and became delirious. As their luck would have it, they stumbled onto a herdsman's summer cabin and David-Néel nursed her son through the night. Yongden's fever broke during the night, and they continued on their way on Christmas day.

The New Year of 1924 found them in Po country. At the outskirts of a village called Sung Zong, a pack of mastiffs, each as big as a small pony, attacked David-Néel. Heinrich Harrer, the author of *Seven Years in Tibet*, once commented, "Their usual diet of milk and calves' flesh gives them enormous strength."[99] David-Néel flailed and jabbed away at them with her staff and beat them off. Shortly afterward, drunken robbers set upon them. A well-placed shot from David-Néel's small revolver and the timely arrival of a group of pilgrims deterred the robbers before the incident turned more violent.

Moving west toward Showa, the capital of Po country, they trod for miles through mysterious forests, gloomy and still. "Then," David-Néel wrote later,

> an unexpected clearing suddenly revealed, behind the dark line of fir trees, extraordinary landscapes of shining snow-clad mountains, towering high in the blue sky, frozen torrents and glittering waterfalls hanging like gigantic and immaculate curtains from the rugged rocks.[100]

The beauty of the country so enchanted the travelers that they loitered in the region for several days, basking in its mild climate and abundant plant life.

Passing through Showa, the two travelers replenished their food supply by begging at the gate of the Po king's dwelling and moved on west toward Giamda. One night, a simply dressed lama showed up unexpectedly in their camp. He sat down and stared at David-Néel. *"Jetsunma* (reverend lady)," he demanded, "why have you removed your rosary and your rings of the initiate? Whom do you expect to fool?"[101]

David-Néel felt that he somehow knew her, but she could not place him. He seemed able to read her thoughts. "You cannot guess, Jetsunma," he half-teased. "I am not who you think and I am anyone you wish."[102] He then engaged David-Néel in a long discussion about Buddhist philosophy and Tibetan mysticism. As he talked, his ideas, his phrasing, and at last his features began to remind her of Sidkeong. Could the lama be an incarnation of her prince? She would never know. The unexpected visitor left as abruptly as he had arrived, but he left her with a sense that he wished her well and had come to bless her visit to Lhasa.

In mid-February, after surviving four months of torturous travel and overcoming one challenge after another, battling brigands, winds and snow, freezing cold, hunger, illness and fever, injuries, and precipitous terrain that suffers inexperienced travelers harshly, David-Néel and her lama son arrived within sight of their destination. "The weather was clear, dry, and cold, the sky luminous," the now 55-year-old woman would write later. "In the rosy light of the rising sun, we sighted the Potala, the huge palace of the lamaist ruler, still far away, yet already majestic and impressive."[103] They quickly closed the remaining distance to Lhasa and entered the city through an intricately carved gate.

POTALA PALACE

Standing in glittering splendor on Mar-po-ri (Red Mountain), 425 feet above the Lhasa River Valley in Lhasa, in what is now the Tibet Autonomous Region in China, the Potala Palace is one of the world's most instantly recognizable landmarks. Just as the Statue of Liberty symbolizes the United States and the Eiffel Tower represents France, the majestic palace stands for Tibet and its Buddhist heritage.

The huge religious and administrative complex contains two major palaces within a palace, the Potrang Karpo, or White Palace, completed in 1648, and the Potrang Marpo, or Red Palace, finished in 1694. Originally, the White Palace served as the seat of the Tibetan government and the home of the Dalai Lama, the religious and civil leader of Tibetan Buddhists. After the mid-eighteenth century, it was used as a winter palace. The Red Palace houses several chapels, innumerable statues of deities and other sacred figures, and the tombs of eight Dalai Lamas. As a religious site, it attracts thousands of Tibetan Buddhists annually.

The original palace complex was built in the seventh century and was later destroyed by the Chinese, but the fifth Dalai Lama ordered it rebuilt on Red Mountain in the seventeenth century. Because of its commanding position above the city, it was used as a major Tibetan military fortress and provided security for the area until the mid-eighteenth century.

The Potala Palace (*Potala* means "Pure Land" or "High Heavenly Realm" in Tibetan) contains 1,000 rooms, more than 200,000 statues, and 10,000 altars. China recognized the palace's value and spared it from destruction when it invaded and occupied Tibet during the Cultural Revolution in 1950. The United Nations Educational, Scientific, and Cultural Organization (UNESCO) named the palace a world heritage site in 1994.

Alexandra David-Néel sits in front of Potala Palace with her adopted son Aphur Yongden and an unidentified youth. David-Néel, who darkened her face with cocoa in order to pass as an Asian, became the first Western woman to enter Lhasa, the Forbidden City, in 1924. As they gazed toward the glittering Potala Palace for the first time within Lhasa, Yongden whispered to David-Néel "*Lha gyalo*"—"the gods win."

Once they stepped inside the city, the air, calm until then, whipped and whirled into a furious sandstorm and lashed them with a great rain of dust. Fortunately for the weary travelers, a young woman offered them shelter from the storm, a room in a beggar's hostel just outside the capital. David-Néel later recalled that the room offered "an extended view of most beautiful scenery, including the Potala." [104]

Yongden lifted his eyes toward the glittering palace. Keeping his voice low so as not to attract unwanted attention, he whispered, *"Lha gyalo"*[105] (the gods win), and so too had Alexandra David-Néel, the first non-Asian woman ever to set foot in the fabled Forbidden City.

9

Stranger in Her Own Land

[W]hen one has been up there [in the Tibetan highlands], there is nothing more to see or do: life—a life like mine, which was nothing more than one long wish to travel—is over; it has achieved its ultimate goal.

—Alexandra David-Néel, in a letter to her husband

David-Néel and Yongden arrived in Lhasa during *Monlam* (festival to celebrate the New Year), and the ongoing festivities enabled them to move around the city more freely than ordinary circumstances might have allowed. They explored the city and nearby points of interest at their leisure and even joined a party of true pilgrims in a tour of the Potala Palace. When David-Néel and Yongden "reached the top of the dominating Potala," as she wrote later, they "enjoyed the beautiful sight of Lhasa, its temples and monasteries lying at our feet like a white, red, and gold carpet spread in the valley."[106] It had taken David-Néel half a lifetime to reach the Forbidden City at the top of the world, but she had picked the perfect time to arrive there:

> I had a happy inspiration when I chose the beginning of the year for my stay at Lhasa, for at any other time it would not have been possible for me to see so many strange festivals and interesting ceremonies. Mingling with the crowds of holiday-makers, I saw cavalcades of gentlemen richly attired in the style of past ages; and cavalry and the infantry of the ancient kings, in their coats of mail, bearing shields and bucklers [a small round shield worn on the left arm], recalling the [Tibet] of former days. There was a certain amount of horseracing. It was disorderly, mad, joyous, and amusing, but not to be compared, from the point of view of horsemanship, with that of the *dokpas* in the Desert of Grass.[107]

David-Néel witnessed great processions of thousands of men parading around the Potala, accompanied by hundreds of embroidered banners, elephants walking gravely, big drums and 15-foot trumpets borne by several men, a variety of Chinese paper monsters, men at arms, and a host of local deities. Lhasa, it seemed, was one great celebration after another, and she relished every moment of her stay there. The city was also home to great poverty, and she lived among the poorest of the poor, where no one "practiced any trade or craft" but "lived, as birds do, on what they could pick up daily." [108]

As the days turned to weeks, David-Néel grew increasingly apprehensive. The threat of discovery posed a continuing risk to the two foreigners. Moreover, she was growing impatient to tell her story to world. By April, the time had come again to move on. "I left Lhasa as quietly as I had entered, and no one suspected that a foreign woman had lived there for two months." [109] Years later, remembering the pageantry of Lhasa, she revisited in her mind the "[u]nforgettable spectacle which alone repaid me for my for my every fatigue and the myriad dangers that I had faced to behold it." [110]

David-Néel and her loyal companion Yongden followed the caravan trails through the Himalayas into India, where they spent the summer of 1924 at Padang, in the Darjeeling district— in a bungalow provided by French Franciscan missionaries. Offers began pouring in from European and American publishers for her story. In October, David-Néel arranged for her belongings to be shipped to Algeria and wrote to Néel that she was at long last ready to return to his arms, but she needed money. Her long put-upon spouse felt less than exuberant and held out little optimism for a successful resumption of their marriage. Nor was he overly elated about the prospect of her bringing a fully mature Asian male home to share their domicile, but he sent money.

The world acclaimed David-Néel's journey as an extraordinary feat. At 55, she had at last exacted her revenge against the British government for forbidding her access to Tibet and for banishing her from India. After regaining her strength, she sailed for home with Yongden. They arrived in France on May 10, 1925.

France named David-Néel a *chevalier* of the Legion of Honor, and the geographic societies of France and Belgium

Alexandra David-Néel set sail from Calcutta to return to Europe, and her husband, after traveling around Asia for 14 years. Upon her return, David-Néel began publishing accounts of her journey in magazines and even wrote a book, which she entitled *My Journey to Lhasa*.

awarded her gold medals. The British Royal Geographical Society awarded her nothing, pointing out that she was not the first European to reach Lhasa; she was, however, the first

European *woman* to enter the city, which the Society chose to ignore. After a 14-year separation, she finally met with Néel in Marseilles shortly before Christmas 1925.

They exchanged stiff kisses on both cheeks and the essential amenities. David-Néel then extolled the fine qualities of Yongden. "We have been together for 11 years in the wilds," she said. "A number of times we have nearly frozen to death, been set on by savage dogs, beaten off bandits. As a matter of honor, you must help me adopt this boy, who I treat as a son."[111]

"I won't stop you," Néel replied. "I don't think it is a good idea. But I don't uphold an old-fashioned law that demands you obtain my permission."[112] He continued to support her emotionally and financially, but they lived apart.

In 1926, David-Néel published her original account of her Tibetan journey in the magazine *Asia* in five installments. A book version, *My Journey to Lhasa,* followed the next year. Britain's Geographical Society demeaned the book because it does not contain a single map. In the coming years, she would write more than 20 books about Tibet, Buddhism, and her experiences, more than 30 books in all. Her writings influenced the work of numerous authors, not least of which was James Hilton's *Lost Horizon.*

For two years after their arrival in France, David-Néel and Yongden traveled the lecture circuit in Europe. In 1928, while touring in the south of France, David-Néel bought a charming little villa outside the quiet spa town of Digne, 95 miles northwest of Nice. Perched on the side of a hill, it enjoyed a pleasant view of the attractive surroundings. She named it *Samten Dzong* (Fortress of Meditation). The villa in the south of France became a refuge for her writing.

At age 60, with Yongden in residence, she settled in at Samten Dzong for almost a decade of productive work: *Magic and Mystery in Tibet* (1929); *Initiations and Initiates in Tibet* (1930); *The Superhuman Life of Gesar of Ling* (1931), the retelling of a Tibetan legend; *Buddhism: Its Doctrines and Its Methods* (1936); and numerous lesser works. She suffered recurring episodes of neurasthenia, and in an effort to fight off the malady, often wrote up to 16 hours a day. Despite her age and illnesses, her traveling days were far from finished.

In the mid-1930s, while still at Digne, David-Néel spent three years raising funds through her book royalties and a grant from the French Ministry of Education to finance her long-planned return to China. On January 9, 1937, David-Néel and Yongden entrained at Gare du Nord in Paris, bound for Berlin, Warsaw, Moscow, and the Far East. Although Néel remained David-Néel's friend and supporter, these two curious partners in a marriage never lived together again.

At age 68, the aging explorer's new and last great adventure began with stopovers in Warsaw and Moscow and then resumed with a long train ride across Siberia to Vladivostok. Mother and adopted son arrived at Peking in midwinter of 1936–1937. At the end of June 1937, they moved on to Wutaishan, the sacred mountain of five peaks. As if to summarize her life, David-Néel remarked, "I can leave countless times, but I will never arrive. Not even the last resting place will hold me."[113]

In early July, after a minor scuffle between Chinese and Japanese troops at the Marco Polo Bridge near Peking had escalated into a full-scale war, David-Néel and Yongden wandered around western and southern China near the Tibetan border. Amid the rapidly deteriorating situation, they continued their studies and writing while barely avoiding Japanese bombs and advancing troops. She described the horrors of war in a letter to Néel, and she began writing a book about life in wartime China, which was later published as *Under the Storm Clouds* (1940).

By the time *Storm Clouds* appeared in print in the spring of 1940, World War II had erupted in Europe and France stood on the verge of collapse. The German war machine rolled into Paris on June 14, and France fell eight days later. Néel, who was now retired, was living in Gard, in the south of France, under the Vichy government, the French collaborationist regime. Meanwhile, his itinerant spouse and her adopted son continued to stay one step ahead of the Japanese invaders in China.

David-Néel and Yongden fled first to Taiyuan to the south, then to Chunking, and on to Chengtu. They finally settled in for most of the war at the frontier town of Tachienlu, within reach of the French consul, Catholic missionaries, and, most important, the post office, her vital link with Mouchy. Soon after David-Néel's arrival in Tachienlu, she received a letter from Néel. He advised her of his will, and he spoke of his gratitude for all the help that Yongden was providing for David-Néel. She had worried continually over Néel's health and safety under the German occupation and had even experienced a premonition of his imminent death.

On February 14, 1941, David-Néel received a telegram from Néel's niece, Simone. When she saw the telegram, she knew its contents without reading it: Néel had died. Part of David-Néel died with him. Tears welled up in the eyes of this woman, who had worked diligently since childhood to conceal her emotions, and she wept openly. Yongden watched his mother with amazement at the sight of her unashamed expression of emotion. "I have lost the best of husbands and my only friend,"[114] David-Néel said. She immersed herself in her work to purge her grief, but her life would never again be the same without her dear Mouchy.

For a time, David-Néel turned bitter, and took out her rancor on poor Yongden, her only remaining loved-one. To escape her hostility, her loyal companion, who had previously abstained from hard drink, began spending more and more time in the local beer parlors. In this way, Yongden adopted a habit that would profoundly affect his future and perhaps his next life.

The intrepid travelers remained as paying guests of the French-Catholic hospital at Tachienlu from 1938 through mid-1944. Finally, caught in the path of Japan's last desperate offensive in China, they moved back to Chengtu. John

ASIAN INCIDENTS

Japan's direct aggression in East Asia began on September 18, 1931. In what came to be known as the "Manchurian Incident," the Japanese Kwantung Army claimed that Chinese soldiers had attempted to bomb a South Manchurian Railway train. The train arrived safely at its destination, but Japanese soldiers quickly seized and occupied the Manchurian city of Mukden, now Shenyang, without authorization from Tokyo, and soon thereafter occupied all of Manchuria. The civilian government in Tokyo lacked the power to control the army, and Japanese military extremists established the "independent state" of Manchukuo, with a puppet government controlled by the Kwantung Army.

On the night of July 7, 1937, the leader of a small Japanese force on maneuvers near the Marco Polo Bridge, outside Peking (now Beijing), demanded entry at the gates of the small walled city of Wanping, now Lugouqiao. Ostensibly, he wanted to search for one of his missing soldiers. The Chinese commander of the Wanping garrison refused entry to the Japanese. A shot rang out, and both sides commenced firing. Soldiers on both sides fell dead.

Diplomatic attempts to ameliorate the clash that the Japanese euphemistically call the "China Incident," but which the Chinese more realistically refer to as their "War of Resistance," failed. The brief exchange of gunfire at Wanping soon escalated into what many military observers recognize as the *true* beginning of World War II. In quick order, such "incidents" became commonplace in Asia, and Alexandra David-Néel found herself in the middle of many of them.

Blofeld, a noted author and Buddhist, visited David-Néel and Yongden in Chengtu and later described it as

> a walled gray-bricked city affectionately styled little Peking. Its residential lanes bordered by low [gray] walls pierced with bronze-studded lacquered gates . . . and the charming courtyards lying behind produced a sometimes startling resemblance to the empress of cities [Peking].[115]

Because David-Néel's living accommodations appeared to Blofeld and others to be quite comfortable, if not sumptuous, and because she appeared to have no identifiable means of support, some of her detractors have speculated that she might have been in the employ of the Vichy government as a spy. Such speculations seem to have died an unsubstantiated death. Whatever the case, while David-Néel and Yongden were still in Chengtu, they learned of the end of World War II in Europe. Germany's surrender in May 1945 also meant the end of the Vichy government. Now, with just three months left in the war in the east, the travelers began preparing for their return to Samten Dzong.

During eight years in China, David-Néel completed a grammar on spoken Tibetan, and then, when forced to leave many of her reference books behind in Peking, she turned to fiction. She produced several novels, including *Mipam* or *The Lama of Five Wisdoms,* and *Tale of Love and Magic.* The experiences that she had stowed in her memory during 24 years of wandering would provide enough material to fuel her creative processes for the rest of her long life.

In late July 1945, David-Néel and Yongden flew to Kunming and then to Calcutta at the expense of the new French government. On June 30, 1946, after enduring eight years in war-wracked China, the indomitable Frenchwoman and her adopted son left the Far East and flew home to France.

David-Néel once wrote that while in Asia, "I delightedly forgot Western lands, that I belonged to them, and that they would probably take me again in the clutches of their sorrowful civilization."[116] How sad David-Néel must have felt when the airplane lifted her off the soil of Asia for the last time and turned to the west; in her heart, she was a stranger in her own land.

10

Together Again

Mrs. David-Néel shut herself away for the last 24 years in
a secluded southern villa, crammed with Buddhist statues,
masks, and prayer wheels.
—From the obituary in the *International Herald Tribune*,
September 9, 1969

After a short stopover in Paris, David-Néel and Yongden returned to Digne. This remarkable woman of 77 years had crammed enough adventure into her seven-plus decades to fill several average lifetimes. The god of longevity continued to grant her daily breath for many years to come, and she made the most of them, researching, writing, translating sacred texts, and spanning the chasm between Eastern religions and Western understanding and acceptance. Arguably, the well-traveled student of religions became the foremost Western authority on Buddhism of her time.

David-Néel exchanged her walking staff for a sturdy cane, and she and her lama son resumed the pedestrian existence of housebound scholars in the quaint spa town in southern France. After making some minor repairs on Samten Dzong, which was slightly damaged during the German occupation, the two travelers again settled in to a routine of research and writing. David-Néel did indulge herself slightly with the purchase of a Citroën, mostly just to move around town. Yongden chauffeured her and she became known locally as "the wife of the Chinese."[117]

In 1947, David-Néel published *A l'ouest barbare de la vaste Chine* (*In China's Wild West*), a study of the frontier lands and the people who lived there. The noted explorer Lowell Thomas, Jr. commented that David-Néel "was a keen observer [who] learned a great deal about China's far west and the intrigues of the border country."[118] Based on her knowledge of China gained by personal experience, she predicted that the Communist forces of Mao Tse-tung would eventually emerge as victors over the nationalist armies of Chiang Kai-shek and that the Communists would go on to rule China.

In 1949, David-Néel published *Nepal: The Heart of the Himalayas,* followed by *India Yesterday, Today and Tomorrow* in 1951. Neither book achieved financial success or was translated into English. In 1954, David-Néel and Yongden published *The Power of Nothingness,* another fictional collaboration based on a Tibetan folk tale. Janwillem van de Wetering, the erudite Buddhist mystery novelist who translated *Nothingness* into English, called it "a novel of suspense" and "a thriller,"[119] and described it this way:

> It has all the elements: a murder, a criminal, a private eye. And it's written the other way around, like some of the modern mysteries that are popular now. You find out who has done it at once and then follow the detective.[120]

Even when collaborating on a mystery novel, David-Néel looked at the world from a perspective all her own. Given more time, this pair might have combined their talents on many more gripping "thrillers," but karma intervened. As arthritis began to erode David-Néel's otherwise good spirits, Yongden, as he had in China, started frequenting the local cafés and increasingly imbibed to escape his mother's increasing displays of ill-humor. With every drink he took, Yongden's end drew closer.

One night in early October 1955, a frantic knocking on David-Néel's door aroused her from sleep. In her half-awake state, her thoughts recalled an old Tibetan superstition: "Death knocks to seek entrance." She refused to answer, but the pounding at her door kept up. "Monsieur is very ill!"[121] a voice called out. Something was wrong with Yongden. David-Néel responded and immediately summoned a physician to attend him. Unhappily, her call for help came too late. David-Néel's faithful Yongden died a few hours later.

Lama Yongden died of uremia, an accumulation of toxic-producing constituents in the blood that are usually eliminated in the urine. Uprooted from his homeland and deeply depressed, he died an alcoholic. Yongden's remains were cremated and held in a vase at Samten Dzong to await the passing of his adoptive mother, friend, and collaborator.

At age 86, David-Néel had lost her staunch companion of the past 40 years, as well as the heir to her estate and literary work. She never fully recovered from the shock of losing her beloved son. Without him, she never wrote another significant book about the Far East. Her oeuvre already included more than 30 books and countless shorter works, which she continued to write for financial gain and to uphold her professional reputation.

With Yongden gone, David-Néel soon found herself in need of household help and companionship. In 1959, she hired Marie-Madeleine Peyronnet, who was known as "Marie-Ma." David-Néel and Marie-Ma represented an interesting study in contrasts: David-Néel, Paris-born and liberal, and Marie-Ma, a *pied noir* (person of European origin living in Algeria under French rule), the product of a military family and conservative upbringing. The two opposites somehow worked out their differences, and Marie-Ma, originally hired as a housekeeper, ultimately became the custodian of David-Néel's home and estate, editor of her posthumous works, and sustainer of her memory.

For the next decade, David-Néel worked on her memoirs, rewrites of some of her earlier books, and *Four Thousand Years of Chinese Expansion,* in which she accurately predicted China's rise as a world power. Despite her growing infirmity, she also played host to hordes of curiosity seekers, hippies, orientalists, and writers, including Lawrence Durrell, author of *The Alexandria Quartet,* who referred to her as that "most astonishing woman,"[122] as well as some royal visitors such as Queen Elizabeth of Belgium and Prince Pierre of Greece.

At age 100, David-Néel decided to renew her passport "just in case."[123] Her mind still entertained notions of returning to Asia, after which she planned a visit to America, but her aged body could no longer support such illusions.

France honored David-Néel on her one-hundredth birthday, elevating her to *commandeur* (commander) of the French Legion of Honor, its highest order. Tibetans accorded her the title of *Jetsunma*, connoting a reincarnated Tibetan saint. Tenzin Gyatso, the fourteenth Dalai Lama, praised her: "We have read her books and we recognize there our own Tibet."[124] The town of Digne named a secondary school after her.

When the French government cast a bronze medal in her image, David-Néel chose the motto for the back of it from Ecclesiastes: "Walk straight on following your heart's desire."[125] Few poets could imagine seven words more appropriate to her life's story.

David-Néel apparently foresaw her end in July 1969. She called Marie-Ma to her bedside and told her that God had spoken to her and illuminated her soul. Then, in a line borrowed from Anatole France's *Thaïs,* she said, "I have seen the nothingness of all that was myself."[126] She embarked on her greatest adventure a month later.

David-Néel died at 3:00 A.M. on September 8, 1969, at Samten Dzong, with Marie-Ma at her bedside, 44 days shy of her 101st birthday. The centenarian's remains were cremated and kept with Yongden's until the ashes of both could be transported to the River Ganges for scattering. Marie-Madeleine carried out the wishes of her mistress at Benares on February 28, 1973. As Janwillem van de Wetering pointed out, "The source of that venerable river lies in Alexandra's beloved Tibet."[127] Home was the hunter after a century of searching her outer and inner worlds for the meaning of existence.

The karmic path to deliverance winds far and long, and the wheel of life spins on. Perhaps elements of Alexandra David-Néel and her adopted Tibetan son have already reunited in another life to resume their journey to nirvana, together again. As David-Néel herself once put it, "What is cannot cease to be."[128]

Chronology

1868 Alexandra Louise Eugénie Alexandrine Marie David is born in Paris on October 24.

1888–1890 David visits England to investigate the Society of the Supreme Gnosis in London. She returns to France and discovers Buddhism and other eastern philosophies at the Theosophical Society and elsewhere in Paris.

1891 She embarks on her first journey to India.

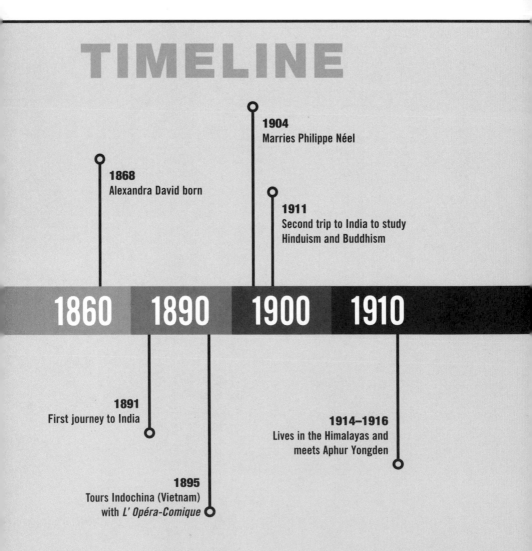

TIMELINE

1904
Marries Philippe Néel

1868
Alexandra David born

1911
Second trip to India to study
Hinduism and Buddhism

1860 **1890** **1900** **1910**

1891
First journey to India

1914–1916
Lives in the Himalayas and
meets Aphur Yongden

1895
Tours Indochina (Vietnam)
with *L' Opéra-Comique*

1895 David tours Indochina (Vietnam) as the lead singer for the road company of *L'Opéra-Comique.*

1898 David publishes *Pour la vie* (*For Life*), a radical treatise advocating free thought and action.

1904 David marries Philippe Néel in Tunis, Tunisia. Louis David, her father, dies in Belgium.

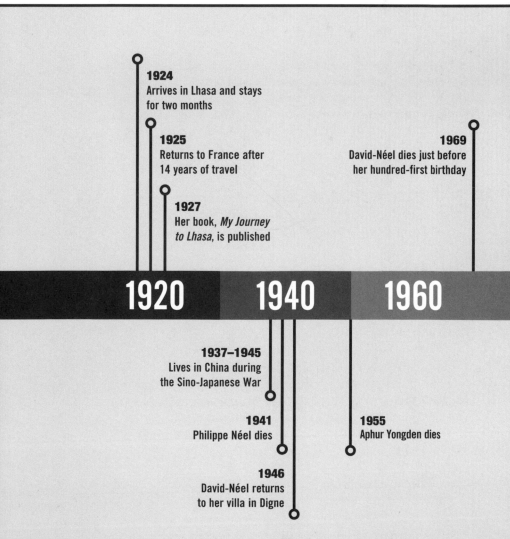

1924
Arrives in Lhasa and stays for two months

1925
Returns to France after 14 years of travel

1927
Her book, *My Journey to Lhasa*, is published

1969
David-Néel dies just before her hundred-first birthday

1920 1940 1960

1937–1945
Lives in China during the Sino-Japanese War

1941
Philippe Néel dies

1955
Aphur Yongden dies

1946
David-Néel returns to her villa in Digne

Chronology

1911 David-Néel departs on her second trip to India to study Hinduism and Buddhism.

1912 She meets Prince Sidkeong Tulku of Sikkim, visits Tibet briefly, and meets the Dalai Lama twice.

1914–1916 David-Néel lives as a hermit high in the Himalayas and studies Buddhism as the disciple of the *gomchen* of Lachen. She meets Yongden, a young Tibetan whom she later adopts as her son.

1917 She tours Japan and Korea with Yongden, who accompanies her everywhere for the rest of his life.

1918–1920 She lives and works among the monks of Kum Bum monastery in eastern Tibet.

1920–1923 David-Néel wanders throughout western China, in the Gobi Desert, and along the Tibetan frontier.

1923 David-Néel leaves French mission on the Mekong River on a four-month journey by foot to the Tibetan capital of Lhasa.

1924 She arrives in Lhasa and stays for two months.

1925 She returns to France.

1927 *My Journey to Lhasa* is published.

1928–1936 She buys a villa (Samten Dzong) in Digne in the south of France and resides and works there, publishing several more books.

1937–1945 David-Néel lives in China during the Sino-Japanese War.

1941 Philippe Néel dies in France.

1946 David-Néel returns to her villa in Digne.

1955 Yongden dies.

1959 David-Néel hires Marie-Madeleine "Marie-Ma" Peyronnet as housekeeper and personal secretary.

1968 Digne celebrates David-Néel's one-hundredth birthday.

1969 David-Néel dies at Digne on September 8, six weeks shy of her 101st birthday.

Notes

Chapter 1

1. Alexandra David-Néel, *My Journey to Lhasa*. Boston: Beacon Press, 1993, p. 153.

2. Ibid., p. 154.

3. Ibid.

4. Ibid.

5. Ibid., p. 156.

6. Ibid.

7. Ibid.

8. Ibid.

9. Ibid., p. 159.

Chapter 2

10. Quoted in Ruth Middleton, *Alexandra David-Néel: Portrait of an Adventurer*. Boston: Shambhala, 1989, p. 2.

11. Ibid.

12. Quoted in Rebecca Stefoff, *Women of the World: Women Travelers and Explorers*. Extraordinary Explorers series. New York: Oxford University Press, 1992, p. 92.

13. Barbara Foster and Michael Foster, *The Secret Lives of Alexandra David-Néel: A Biography of the Explorer of Tibet and Its Forbidden Practices*. New York: Overlook Press, 1998, p. 11.

14. Ibid., p. 12.

15. Quoted in *Summary Biography of Alexandra David-Néel*, http://www.alexandra-david-neel.org/anglais/biog2.htm, p. 2.

16. Quoted in Middleton, *Alexandra David-Néel*, p. 8.

17. Ibid., p. 7.

18. Ibid., p. 11.

19. Ibid., p. 14.

20. Quoted in Foster and Foster, *Secret Lives*, p. 24.

21. Ibid., p. 25.

22. Quoted in *Summary Biography of Alexandra David-Néel*, http://www.alexandra-david-neel.org/anglais/biog3.htm, p. 1.

Chapter 3:

23. Quoted in Middleton, *Alexandra David-Néel*, p. 18.

24. Ibid.

25. Foster and Foster, *Secret Lives*, p. 30.

26. Ibid., pp. 29–30.

27. Quoted in Middleton, *Alexandra David-Néel*, p. 23.

28. Ibid., p. 25.

29. Ibid., p. 27.

30. Quoted in Foster and Foster, *Secret Lives*, p. 35.

31. Ibid., p. 33.

32. Quoted in *Summary Biography of Alexandra David-Néel*, http://www.alexandra-david-neel.org/anglais/biog4.htm, p. 2.

Chapter 4

33. Middleton, *Alexandra David-Néel*, p. 33.

34. Foster and Foster, *Secret Lives*, p. 42.

35. Quoted in Middleton, *Alexandra David-Néel*, p. 32.

36. Ibid., p. 35.

37. Ibid., p. 36.

38. Quoted in Stefoff, *Women of the World*, p. 94.

39. Quoted in Middleton, *Alexandra David-Néel*, p. 40.

40. Ibid., p. 42.

41. Ibid.

Chapter 5

42. Quoted in Middleton, *Alexandra David-Néel*, p. 44.

43. Alexandra David-Néel, *Buddhism: Its Doctrines and Its Methods* (Kathmandu, Nepal: Pilgrims Book House, 2000, pp. 175–76.

44. Quoted in Foster and Foster, *Secret Lives*, p. 53.

45. Ibid., p. 54.

46. Quoted in Middleton, *Alexandra David-Néel*, p. 49.

47. Quoted in Diana N. Rowan, new introduction to David-Néel, *My Journey to Lhasa*, p. xviii.

48. Quoted in Foster and Foster, *Secret Lives of Alexandra David-Néel*, p. 85.

49. Alexandra David-Néel, *Magic and Mystery in Tibet*. New York: Dover, 1971, p. 2.

50. Ibid., p. 4.

51. Ibid., p. 2.

52. Quoted in Middleton, *Alexandra David-Néel*, p. 57.

53. Quoted in Foster and Foster, *Secret Lives*, p. 66.

54. David-Néel, *Magic and Mystery in Tibet*, p. 1.

55. Middleton, *Alexandra David-Néel*, p. 58.

56. Ibid.

57. Quoted in Middleton, *Alexandra David-Néel*, p. 70.

58. Ibid., p. 96.

Chapter 6

59. David-Néel, *Magic and Mystery in Tibet*, p. 42.

60. Ibid., p. 75.

61. Quoted in Foster and Foster, *Secret Lives*, p. 123.

62. Ibid., pp. 123–24.

63. Ibid., p. 129.

64. Alexandra David-Néel and Lama Yongden, *The Secret Oral Teachings in Tibetan Buddhist Sects*. Translated by Captain H. N. M. Hardy. San Francisco: City Lights Books, 1967, p. 123.

65. Quoted in Foster and Foster, *Secret Lives*, p. 134.

66. David-Néel, *My Journey to Lhasa*, p. xxxvi.

67. Foster and Foster, *Secret Lives*, p. 137.

68. Quoted in *Summary Biography of Alexandra David-Néel*, http://www.alexandra-david-neel.org/anglais/biog5.htm, p. 3

69. Ibid.

Chapter 7

70. David-Néel, *Magic and Mystery in Tibet*, p. 93.

71. Ibid.

72. Quoted in Middleton, *Alexandra David-Néel*, p. 119.

73. Ibid., p. 120.

74. Quoted in Foster and Foster, *Secret Lives*, p. 146.

Notes

75. Ibid.

76. Ibid.

77. Quoted in Tiziana and Gianni Baldizzone, *Tibet: Journey to the Forbidden City: Retracing the Steps of Alexandra David-Néel*. New York: Stewart, Tabori and Chang, 1996, p. 20.

78. Quoted in Foster and Foster, *Secret Lives*, p. 151.

79. David-Néel, *Magic and Mystery in Tibet*, p. 119.

80. Quoted in Milbry Polk and Mary Tiegreen, *Women of Discovery: A Celebration of Intrepid Women Who Explored the World*. New York: Clarkson Potter, 2001, 69.

Chapter 8

81. Quoted in Middleton, *Alexandra David-Néel*, p. 137.

82. Quoted in Baldizzone and Baldizzone, *Tibet*, p. 12.

83. Quoted in Foster and Foster, *Secret Lives*, p. 174.

84. David-Néel, *My Journey to Lhasa*, p. 1.

85. Quoted in Don Brown, *Far Beyond the Garden Gate: Alexandra David-Néel's Journey to Lhasa*. Boston: Houghton Mifflin, 2002, p. 14.

86. Ibid., p. 16.

87. Quoted in Middleton, *Alexandra David-Néel*, p. 160.

88. Quoted in Brown, *Far Beyond the Garden Gate*, p. 16.

89. Quoted in Foster and Foster, *Secret Lives*, p. 189.

90. Quoted in Middleton, *Alexandra David-Néel*, p. 160.

91. Quoted in Foster and Foster, *Secret Lives*, p. 192.

92. David-Néel, *My Journey to Lhasa*, p. 90.

93. Ibid., p. 91.

94. Ibid.

95. Ibid., p. 92.

96. Ibid.

97. Ibid.

98. Ibid., p. 162.

99. Quoted in Foster and Foster, *Secret Lives*, p. 205.

100. David-Néel, *My Journey to Lhasa*, p. 194.

101. Quoted in Foster and Foster, *Secret Lives*, p. 208.

102. Ibid., p. 209.

103. David-Néel, *My Journey to Lhasa*, p. 255.

104. Ibid., p. 258.

105. Ibid.

Chapter 9

106. David-Néel, *My Journey to Lhasa*, p. 265.

107. Ibid., p. 282.

108. Ibid., p. 285.

109. Ibid., p. 298.

110. Ibid., p. 297

111. Quoted in Foster and Foster, *Secret Lives*, p. 238.

112. Ibid.

113. Ibid., p. 259.

114. Quoted in *Summary Biography of Alexandra David-Néel,* http://www.alexandra-david-neel.org/anglais/biog7.htm, p. 1.

115. Quoted in Foster and Foster, *Secret Lives,* p. 275.

116. Quoted in Sidonie Smith, *Moving Lives: Twentieth-Century Women's Travel Writing.* Minneapolis: University of Minnesota Press, 2001, 44.

Chapter 10

117. Quoted in Foster and Foster, *Secret Lives,* p. 279.

118. Ibid., p. 278.

119. Quoted in Janwillem van de Wetering, introduction to *The Power of Nothingness,* by Alexandra David-Néel and Lama Yongden. Translated by Janwillem van de Wetering. Boston: Houghton Mifflin, 1982, pp. xiv–xv.

120. Ibid., p. xiv.

121. Quoted in Middleton, *Alexandra David-Néel,* p. 179.

122. Quoted in Foster and Foster, *Secret Lives,* p. 286.

123. Quoted in Middleton, *Alexandra David-Néel,* p. 179.

124. Quoted in Foster and Foster, *Secret Lives,* p. 293.

125. Quoted in Polk and Tiegreen, *Women of Discovery,* p. 69.

126. Quoted in Foster and Foster, *Secret Lives,* p. 296.

127. Quoted in Wetering, *The Power of Nothingness,* p. xv.

128. Alexandra David-Néel, *Immortality and Reincarnation.* Translated by Jon Graham. Rochester, VT: Inner Traditions, 1997, p. 128.

Bibliography

Books

Baldizzone, Tiziana, and Gianni Baldizzone. *Tibet: Journey to the Forbidden City: Retracing the Steps of Alexandra David-Néel.* New York: Stewart, Tabori and Chang, 1996.

Bowker, John, ed. *The Oxford Dictionary of World Religions.* New York: Oxford University Press, 1997.

Brown, Don. *Far Beyond the Garden Gate: Alexandra David-Néel's Journey to Lhasa.* Boston: Houghton Mifflin, 2002.

David-Néel, Alexandra. *Buddhism: Its doctrines and Its methods.* Kathmandu, Nepal: Pilgrims Book House, 2000.

———. *Immortality and Reincarnation.* Translated by Jon Graham. Rochester, Vt.: Inner Traditions, 1997.

———. *My Journey to Lhasa.* Boston: Beacon Press, 1993.

———. *Initiations and Initiates in Tibet.* New York: Dover, 1993.

———. *Magic and Mystery in Tibet.* New York: Dover, 1971.

David-Néel, Alexandra, and Lama Yongden. *The Power of Nothingness.* Translated by Janwillem van de Wetering. Boston: Houghton Mifflin, 1982.

———. *The Secret Oral Teachings in Tibetan Buddhist Sects.* Translated by Capt. H.N.M. Hardy. San Francisco: City Lights Books, 1967.

Doniger, Wendy, ed. *Merriam-Webster's Encyclopedia of World Religions.* Springfield, Mass.: Merriam-Webster, 1999.

Foster, Barbara, and Michael Foster. *The Secret Lives of Alexandra David-Néel: A Biography of the Explorer of Tibet and Its Forbidden Practices.* New York: Overlook Press, 1998.

Fraisse, Geneviève, and Michelle Perrot, eds. *A History of Women in the West.* Vol. IV. *Emerging Feminism from Revolution to World War.* Georges Duby and Michelle Perrot, general editors. Cambridge, Mass.: Belknap Press of Harvard University Press, 1993.

Gard, Richard A., ed. *Buddhism.* Great Religions of Modern Man series. New York: George Braziller, 1962.

Johnson, Gordon. *Cultural Atlas of India: India, Pakistan, Nepal, Bhutan, Bangladesh and Sri Lanka.* New York: Facts On File, 1996.

McLoone, Margo. *Women Explorers in Asia: Lucy Atkinson, Alexandra David-Néel, Dervla Murphy, Susie Carson Rijnhart, Freya Stark.* Mankato, Minn.: Capstone Press, 1997.

Meyer, Karl E., and Shareen Blair Brysac. *Tournament of Shadows: The Great Game and the Race for Empire in Central Asia.* Washington, D.C.: Counterpoint, 1999.

Middleton, Ruth. *Alexandra David-Neel: Portrait of an Adventurer.* Boston: Shambhala, 1989.

O'Reilly, James, and Larry Habegger. *Tibet: True Stories.* San Francisco: Travelers' Tales, 2003.

Oxford Atlas of Exploration. New York: Oxford University Press, 1997.

Polk, Milbry, and Mary Tiegreen. *Women of Discovery: A Celebration of Intrepid Women Who Explored the World.* New York: Clarkson Potter, 2001.

Renou, Louis, ed. *Hinduism.* Great Religions of Modern Man series. New York: George Braziller, 1962.

Smith, Huston. *The World's Religions: Our Great Wisdom Traditions.* New York: HarperCollins, 1991.

Smith, Sidonie. *Moving Lives: Twentieth-Century Women's Travel Writing.* Minneapolis: University of Minnesota Press, 2001.

Stefoff, Rebecca. *Women of the World: Women Travelers and Explorers.* Extraordinary Explorers series. New York: Oxford University Press, 1992.

Watts, Alan. *Three: The Way of Zen; Nature, Man, and Woman; Psychotherapy East and West.* New York: Pantheon Books, 1961.

Websites

Summary Biography of Alexandra David-Néel. http://www.alexandra-david-neel.org/anglais/biog.htm.

Further Reading

Bohlander, Richard E., ed. *World Explorers and Discoverers*. New York: Da Capo Press, 1998.

Boorstin, Daniel J. *The Discoverers*. New York: Random House, 1983.

Confucius. *The Sayings of Confucius*. Translated by James R. Ware. New York: New American Library, 1955.

Honderich, Ted, ed. *The Oxford Companion to Philosophy*. New York: Oxford University Press, 1995.

Hookam, Hilda. *A Short History of China*. New York: New American Library, 1972.

James, Lawrence. *Raj: The Making and Unmaking of British India*. New York: St. Martin's Press, 1997.

Jansz, Natania, Miranda Davies, Emma Drew, and Lori McDougall, eds. *Women Travel: First-hand Accounts from more than 60 Countries*. London: Rough Guides, 2000.

Kapleau, Philip. *The Wheel of Life: A Practical and Spiritual Guide*. New York: Doubleday, 1989.

Katz, Elizabeth, comp. *India in Pictures*. Visual Geography Series. New York: Sterling Publishing, 1973.

Lao Tzu. *The Way of Life*. Translated by R.B. Blakney. New York: New American Library, 1955.

Novaresio, Paolo. *The Explorers: From the Ancient World to the Present*. New York: Stewart, Tabori and Chang, 1996.

Read, Anthony, and David Fisher. *The Proudest Day: India's Long Road to Independence*. New York: W.W. Norton, 1998.

Sohl, Robert, and Audrey Carr, eds. *The Gospel According to Zen: beyond the death of god*. New York: New American Library, 1970.

Suzuki, D.T. *An Introduction to Zen Buddhism*. New York: Grove Press, 1964.

Trungpa, Chögyam. *Shambhala: The Sacred Path of the Warrior*. New York: Bantam Books, 1984.

Wolpert, Stanley. *A New History of India*. 5th ed. New York: Oxford University Press, 1997.

Yohannan, John D., ed. *A Treasury of Asian Literature*. New York: New American Library, 1956.

Index

Index

Index

lama(s)
  and Blavatsky, 15
  David-Néel as, 47, 56
  David-Néel's writings on,
    31
  red-hat, 46, 52, 71
  yellow-hat, 45-46, 62
  Yongden as, 64-65, 67, 71
"Lamp of Wisdom," as name
  given to David-Néel, 54, 55
Lanchow, China, David-Néel
  traveling through, 68
latsa (prayer flags)
  David-Néel encountering,
    73
  and World War I, 63
Legion of Honor
  David-Néel as *chevalier* of,
    82
  David-Néel as *commandeur*
    of, 94
leopard, David-Néel's
  encounter with, 71
Lhasa (Forbidden City). *See*
  Tibet
Lidia (one-act lyric drama),
  26
Likiang, China, David-Néel
  traveling through, 69
London Buddhist Society,
  David-Néel lecturing before,
  32
long-gom walking, 54
Lost Horizon (James Hilton),
  62, 84
Louis Philipe (the Citizen
  King), 10

Madurai, India, David-Néel in,
  38
Magic and Mystery in Tibet, 54,
  61, 84

Mahayana Buddhism, 45-46,
  52, 54-55
Manchu dynasty, 61
Mao Tse-tung, 91
mastiffs, David-Néel attacked
  by, 75
meditation, David-Néel engag-
  ing in, 64
Mercure de France, David-Néel's
  articles in, 31
middle way, and Buddhism,
  12
Mipam or *The Lama of Five
  Wisdoms*, 88
Miserable, Les (Victor Hugo),
  26
mo (telling fortunes), Yongden
  performing, 71
*Modernisme bouddhiste et le
  bouddhisme du Bouddha, La
  (The Modern Buddhist and
  the Buddhism of Buddha)*,
  33-34
momos (meat wrapped in ball
  of baked paté and steamed),
  63
Mongol heritage, David-Néel's
  claim of, 10
Monlam (festival to celebrate
  New Year), 81-82
Morgan, Elisabeth, 13, 14, 15,
  19, 20
Musée Guimet, David-Néel
  visiting, 17, 19, 21
music
  David-Néel's love of, 12,
    13, 14, 23-24, 26-27, 29-
    30
  of Tibet, 26, 34
My Journey to Lhasa, 69, 84
Myrial, Monsieur and Madame,
  24, 26

Index

Index

Index

Picture Credits

Contributors

....

Earle Rice Jr. is a former senior design engineer and technical writer in the aerospace industry. After serving nine years with the United States Marine Corps, he attended San Jose City College and Foothill College on the San Francisco Peninsula. He has devoted full time to his writing since 1993 and has written more than 40 books for young adults, including 10 books for Chelsea House Publishers. The author is a member of the Society of Children's Book Writers and Illustrators; the League of World War I Aviation Historians and its British-based sister organization, Cross and Cockade International; the United States Naval Institute; and the Air Force Association.

Series consulting editor **Milbry Polk** graduated from Harvard in 1976. An explorer all her life, she has ridden horseback through Pakistan's Northwest Territories, traveled with Bedouin tribesmen in Jordan and Egypt, surveyed Arthurian sites in Wales, and trained for the first Chinese-American canoe expedition. In 1979, supported by the National Geographic Society, Polk led a camel expedition retracing the route of Alexander the Great across Egypt.

Her work as a photojournalist has appeared in numerous magazines, including *Time, Fortune, Cosmopolitan* and *Quest*. Currently she is a contributing editor to the *Explorers Journal*. Polk is a Fellow of the Royal Geographic Society and a Fellow of the Explorers Club. She is the also the author of two award-winning books, *Egyptian Mummies* (Dutton Penguin, 1997) and *Women of Discovery* (Clarkson Potter, 2001).

Milbry Polk serves as an advisor to the George Polk Awards for Journalistic Excellence, is on the Council of the New York Hall of Science, serves on the Board of Governors of the National Arts Club, the Children's Shakespeare Theater Board and is the director of Wings World Quest. She lives in Palisades, New York, with her husband and her three daughters. She and her daughters row on the Hudson River.